Gurus of Chaos
MODERN INDIA'S MONEY MASTERS

Gurus of Chaos

Modern India's Money Masters

Saurabh Mukherjea

B L O O M S B U R Y

LONDON • NEW DELHI • NEW YORK • SYDNEY

BS books]

AN IMPRINT OF BUSINESS STANDARD LIMITED

Bloomsbury Publishing India Pvt Ltd
Vishrut Building, DDA Complex, Building No. 3,
Pocket C-6 & 7, Vasant Kunj, New Delhi 110 070
www.bloomsbury.com

Nehru House, 4 Bahadur Shah Zafar Marg, New Delhi 11 0002
www.business-standard.com/books

ISBN: 978-93-84052-55-3

10 9 8 7 6 5 4

Typeset by Eleven Arts
Keshav Puram, Delhi 110035

Printed and bound by Thomson Press

To the 'home team':
Sarbani, Jeet and Malini

Contents

Foreword

The Indian stock market is many things to many people. Some are drawn to its thrill and promise but more often than not, people fail to understand the risk that runs beside the reward of a great ride. For many, the markets and its workings seem to defy logic and mastery. Whilst all participants in the stock markets seek disproportionate outperformance, uncovering what it takes to be successful in the stock markets is something only a handful of individuals have managed to do.

Six years ago, Saurabh Mukherjea moved to India from the UK after selling the highly rated London-based Institutional Equities research franchise that he had co-founded in his mid-20s. Those were the days when the Indian stock market lacked high quality research other than research prepared by a few select brokers. I got Saurabh on board to help me build Ambit's equities franchise. Today our Institutional Equities business is one of the most respected in the industry with its franchise built around its focus on high quality, high integrity research.

Saurabh's almost obsessive focus on ensuring high quality research has motivated him to write this book. Using the clarity of thought that has become his hallmark, he provides the reader with a clear view on what the drivers behind successful investing are. With over a decade of experience in the stock markets both in India and the UK, Saurabh brings together in this book, not only his learnings, but also the collective wisdom of a small group of India's elite investors. Each of these highly successful long term investors has built for himself a fine set of navigation tools and developed a unique perspective and approach towards the market. The book carries detailed interviews with these investors where they speak freely about their passions, dreams, fears and shortcomings. For the reader this offers a fascinating insight into a world that seemingly operates in mysterious ways.

The book is based on in-depth research using rigorous analytical and forensic accounting techniques, which has now become the guiding principle for every business in Ambit. Saurabh highlights how easy it is to overlook glaring faults in companies' performance and how these can be easily spotted using basic number crunching tools. He also delves deeper into a series of smartly crafted techniques that can be used to uncover serious accounting issues or corporate governance issues that companies might be trying to cover up.

While technical knowledge of the latest research techniques is necessary, it is not a sufficient condition of success in the stock market. Such knowledge has to be combined with a strong work ethic, strength of character, humility and—most importantly—the ability to think differently from others. Focusing in particular on this last aspect, the book highlights how strength of character combined with in-depth knowledge is the foundation of differentiated thinking which in turn helps deliver outstanding long term investment returns. Ironically, those individuals who possess this combination of character strengths are rarely driven by money or greed; their interests in life tend to extend well beyond the stock market and that in turn allows them to invest dispassionately and successfully.

"Gurus of Chaos" is therefore a rare glimpse into the unique minds of elite investors who have consistently delivered, despite the trying conditions of the Indian stock market. I would recommend the book not just to investors but to everyone who is trying to succeed in the increasingly vibrant free market economy that India is gradually becoming. Patience, humility, fortitude and contrarian thinking—these seemingly old fashioned values matter in and outside the stock market and all of us can draw inspiration from the investment gurus who have demonstrated these strengths over the last twenty years. I hope you derive as much value from and as much enjoyment from "Gurus of Chaos" as I did.

Ashok Wadhwa
Group CEO, Ambit Holdings
Mumbai, October 2014

The High Noon of Indian Capitalism

The smog refused to lift even as the ancient Ambassador taxi wheezed its way through the empty streets of Kolkata. It was a chilly January morning and with our five-month-old son, my wife and I were heading to the airport to fly back to London having attended a family function at my ancestral home. The year was 2008.

As we watched the first few office workers get on to buses and trams, the taxi driver asked me in Hindi, *'Reliance Power...sir kya lagta? Company kaisa hai?'* ['What do you think of Reliance Power?']. When I replied that since I didn't live in India, I did not know about Reliance Power, the driver realised that he could help me out. *'Riks kam hai, security zyada hai'* said the driver ['The risk associated with the company is low. It looks like a secure company.'] I chided myself for not having realised that the taxi driver was asking me about Reliance Power's Initial Public Offering (IPO), the largest ever in India, wherein the company was planning to issue to the public shares with a value in excess of ₹100 billion.

By now, in spite of the wintry fog and my son's demands for attention, I was intrigued. I was after all in Kolkata, the capital of a state ruled by a Communist government for nearly 30 years, a city known for its intellectuals and its food but not renowned for its risk appetite. And yet almost every second person I had met in the preceding week was discussing the IPO. The evening before, at the dinner table I heard elderly relatives—lawyers, architects, accountants, executives—discussing amongst themselves how many shares of Reliance Power they might be able to get at the upcoming IPO. My Bengali relatives had never before shown such enthusiasm either for the stock market or for free market enterprise. I was pleasantly surprised but also taken aback by the winds of change sweeping this bastion of Left-wing thought.

I asked the driver a few questions to understand how much he was planning to invest in the IPO. The driver, a migrant from the state of Bihar, earned around ₹100,000 a year. He was hoping to be able to invest ₹20,000 in the IPO. These were the savings he had accumulated over the last couple of years. The previous tranche of savings had been invested in buying a water pump back in his village in Bihar where his wife and children lived with the extended family. He had an account at a local sub-brokerage of a national brokerage chain and the sub-broker had told his customers that this IPO would give investors lucky enough to get shares 40 per cent returns per annum.

A few weeks later, Reliance Power went public on 11 February 2008. I never found out whether the taxi driver was 'lucky enough' to buy shares in Reliance Power's IPO. Several of my relatives did invest in the IPO. They are still trying to figure out what hit them. An investor who bought Reliance Power shares worth ₹100,000 at the IPO, will have at the prices prevalent in August 2014 a mere ₹32,000 worth of shares. That translates into a negative rate of return of 17 per cent per annum in the intervening six and a half years.

In totality, the public invested ₹103 billion in the IPO. Six years later, that ₹103 billion has now become ₹33 billion. Where has the ₹70 billion gone? This after all is a utility company which promised to invest the public's money in power plants. Did those investments actually take place? Or did the government short-change the utility and indulge in post-contractual opportunism? Or are there other factors at play which explain the sub-par post-IPO performance of Reliance Power?

Reliance Power is an extreme version of the sort of issues which make investing in the Indian market so challenging. The investment opportunities in India are so obvious that almost every newspaper reader is aware of them. And yet, the overwhelming majority of Indian companies seem to struggle to turn these opportunities into double digit returns for their shareholders. In fact, over the past 20 years, over 80 per cent of listed Indian companies have failed to give share price returns better than the rate of inflation (which has been around 7 per cent over the period in question). However, whilst the vast majority of companies have failed to generate even double digit shareholder returns, the remaining minority have given healthy returns better than or equal to GDP growth (which has been around 14 per cent, in nominal terms over the past two decades).

These challenges mean that only a very small number of investors in the Indian stock market are able to deliver market beating returns over long periods of time. To deliver such returns they have to excel in investing in that minority of companies which are able to profit from the Indian economy's robust performance over the last 20 years.

Ever since I returned from London to work in the Indian stock market, the success of this elite group of investors has fascinated me. How do they stay calm in the face of mass hysteria over a company's prospects? How are they able to understand which company will deal with politicians and bureaucrats ably and still deliver healthy returns for their shareholders? How are they able to see through the accounting subterfuges that a significant minority of Indian companies resorts to?

This book seeks to shed more light on how the *Gurus of Chaos* in the Indian stock market build their portfolios and, just as importantly, nurture their successful multi-decadal careers in a turbulent market, which to the untrained eye, seems more characterised by risk than by reward.

ONE

10,000 hours

HYDERABAD—POWER, INFRASTRUCTURE AND CONSTRUCTION HAVEN

My family and I moved to India in the summer of 2008 just as the first season of the Indian Premier League was drawing to a close. Although the stock market had already peaked in January 2008, the economy still felt like it was on fire after four years of supercharged economic growth. Having just sold the small London-based equity research business that I had co-founded to a much larger British brokerage firm, I had been sent to Mumbai by my new masters to build their Indian business. As part of my effort to familiarise myself with the country, I decided I would spend a couple of months meeting Indian companies across various sectors. Thus, on a hot summer's day in August 2008 I found myself on a flight to Hyderabad.

I was flying from Mumbai to Hyderabad to meet the Chief Financial Officer (CFO) of one of the leading power and construction companies in the country. With me was my colleague who is an expert on the power sector. Throughout that journey we tried in vain to make sense of that power company's balance sheet, a balance sheet which contained a high quantum of 'loans' in, both, Assets and Liabilities columns. Loans taken by this company amounted to as much as the quantum of its shareholders' equity. Even more interestingly, money lent by the power company amounted to almost twice the amount of its shareholders' equity. Why was it lending so much money? Who was it lending that money to?

Three hours later, we got our answers after questioning the CFO; first politely over lunch and then, more intensively in his office. The listed company (let's call it ListCo) was lending money to various shell companies. Those shell companies then took equity stakes in the power plants that ListCo had won tenders for. Each of these power plants was being managed through a Special Purpose Vehicle (SPV), which then gave the 'construction' order to ListCo. Thus the loans advanced by ListCo were also being accounted for in its profit and loss account (P&L) as revenues and hence profits. Put simply, ListCo was borrowing money from the bank, lending it to itself and then showing it as profit!

These profits that ListCo showed on its P&L obviously boosted its shareholders' equity. That in turn allowed ListCo to borrow more money from the banks which in turn allowed it to finance more power plants (for which the construction order would of course come to ListCo). Thus this insane spiral, which looked to me to be a contravention of any sane accounting standard, continued. (I found out later that the company was, in effect, contravening what is called Accounting Standard 21.)

It took me another month to understand the full extent of such accounting shenanigans not just in the company in question but more generally in the utilities, infrastructure, construction and real estate sectors in India. In the years that followed, as investors who followed my line of thought lost faith in the financial statements and business models of these companies, their share prices plummeted. At its peak in 2008 these four sectors accounted for 20 per cent (or ₹14.5 trillion) of the market capitalisation of the Indian stock market. Now, in August 2014, they account for only 10 per cent (or ₹9.3 trillion) of the market, implying that those who owned shares in these sectors in 2008 have lost more than ₹5 trillion (around US$100 billion) of their wealth.

What is even more interesting than the accounting shenanigans of the power, infrastructure, construction and real estate companies is the fact that in those heady days most investors did not seem to care about these manoeuvres. In fact, many fund managers understood the fictitious nature of these company's accounts; yet they were itching to buy more stock in these companies.

However, even at the height of this frenzy that gripped India between 2007 and 2010, there was a small minority of investors who decided to steer clear of these sectors. For someone like myself who had just landed in India, what made the restraint of this tiny subset of investors even more admirable was the fact that they avoided the 'hot' sectors at a time when:

- the CEOs in these sectors were being lionised on the cover pages of business magazines;
- the average fund manager was pouring money into these sectors (and reaping the short term rewards from those investments); and
- the marketing departments of various fund management houses were falling over themselves to launch 'India Infrastructure Funds'.

Such level headedness practiced over multiple decades in an emerging market characterised by misleading accounting, multi-faceted corruption and low liquidity (India is by far the least liquid of the world's fifteen largest stock markets[1]) is the province of a select few individuals. This book is about such mindsets of such individuals. It delves into their psyche, their careers and their evolution as successful long-term investors. In its final chapter,

---

[1] Liquidity for a stock is usually measured by how much trading (measured in US$ million) takes place in that counter on a daily basis. This is called the Average Daily Value or ADV. "ADV: Market Cap" is a therefore a simple measure of how liquid a stockmarket is. Most large stockmarkets have a ratio of around 0.30 per cent i.e. 0.30 per cent of the market cap is being traded in that market on a daily basis. For India, the corresponding figure, in February 2014, was 0.20 per cent even if we sum up the liquidity on the NSE and the BSE.

the book asks whether you and I can invest as successfully as this elite minority does.

THE ANTIDOTE TO HYDERABAD COMES FROM WORLI

Once upon a time in Mumbai, there used to be a flourishing synthetic textiles company called Nirlon. At the height of the 'license Raj' in the 1970s and the early 1980s, Nirlon used to manufacture nylon polyester and nylon tyrecord. To deploy some of the surplus cash its businesses were throwing off, the company constructed a high rise office building in Worli and named it Nirlon House. Unfortunately, from the late 1980s onwards, Nirlon's fortunes began to slide due to excess production in India of synthetic textiles and due to the end of the 'license Raj' in 1991. Nirlon was officially deemed a sick company in 1988 and it wasn't until 2006 that the company was able to shake off this tag.

However, even as Nirlon's fortunes slid in the late 1980s, in Nirlon House a remarkable company was born. In 1988, in this nondescript building in Worli, Crisil was created. Although Crisil, a leading credit rating agency in India, is now headquartered in a beautiful, custom built property twenty miles away in Powai, it was in Nirlon House in the late 1980s that Pradip Shah, the first Managing Director of the firm, laid the foundations of this remarkable institution. In so doing, he brought modern credit research to India and, in effect, lit the spark for the creation of a functional corporate bond market in India.

Mr Shah, a powerhouse who has influenced several modern day finance professionals, was not alone; in the late 1980s and early 1990s, several remarkable men and women joined Crisil and were amongst the first people in India to learn how to professionally analyse financial statements and how to rate companies. One such young talent was Sanjoy Bhattacharya, who in 2000 went on to become the founding Chief Investment Officer of HDFC Asset Management, now India's largest mutual fund house with over ₹1 trillion under management.

Prior to joining Crisil, Sanjoy already had four years of experience of market research at MARG, a reputed market research firm, preceded by an MBA from IIM (Ahmedabad). But it was in Crisil that in 1988 Sanjoy found his guru and his calling in life. Twenty years after he had left Crisil, Sanjoy told me that Pradip Shah's role in his life had been invaluable.

When asked what exactly influenced the young IIM graduate, Sanjoy replied: 'He (Pradip Shah) said "please learn from your mistakes I have no problem if you guys make mistakes. Don't repeat them." All of us at Crisil benefited because of this attitude. After studying a company for a couple of days, I would think I had learnt something. Then I would meet Pradip to brief him on the company and agree upon what we should ask the promoter. Pradip would indulge me for 15 minutes and then ask me three questions which would make it obvious that, compared to him, I really knew nothing about the company.' Sanjoy emphatically says that the years he spent at Crisil shaped his analytical skills. He learnt the importance of being rigorous, comprehensive and sceptical when reviewing business data. His years at Crisil followed by the years that Sanjoy has spent meeting company promoters and analysing financial statements has given him the sort of training in finance that money cannot buy.

This sort of relentless application in the formative days of their career under the tutelage of a master or in the confines of a progressive organisation is a common feature of many of the master investors featured in this book. In fact, as American author Malcolm Gladwell and British table tennis champ turned author Matthew Syed have shown, this pattern of prolonged purposeful training under an enlightened guru is a hallmark of success across different fields. In his provocative book, *Outliers: The Story of Success*, Gladwell overturned our conventional view of success that it is mostly about the innate talent possessed by almost superhuman individuals. Using examples as diverse as Bill Gates, the Beatles, Canadian ice hockey players and Jewish lawyers in New York, Gladwell made the point that success arises from a mixture of immense application—usually, many thousands of hours of practice—and social circumstances, for example, being born to the 'right' parents, in the 'right' place and at the 'right' time. Matthew Syed applies the same line of thought to sport.

In his inspirational book, *Bounce: The Myth of Talent and the Power of Practice*, Matthew Syed takes Gladwell's thinking and extends it. Syed, a former UK number 1 table tennis player, debunks many of our cherished myths about talented super-achievers. Using examples ranging from chess players to violinists to firefighters, Syed highlights that success arises from:

- **10,000 hours of practice**: '...from art to science and from board games to tennis, it has been found that a minimum of ten years is required to reach world-class status in any complex task...In *Outliers*, Malcolm Gladwell points out that most top performers practice for around one thousand hours per year... so he re-describes the ten-year rule as the ten-thousand hour rule. This is the minimum time necessary for the acquisition of expertise in any complex task.'[2]
- The **guidance of coaches and institutions** which encourages 'purposeful practice'. The whole process of learning and growing becomes more efficient if done under the tutelage of experts who can spot the budding star's mistakes and supply remedies whilst harnessing his or her strengths.
- An **enabling environment** which gives the stars of tomorrow access to both of the above. Without this environment and the opportunities that it creates, we would not have the Sachin Tendulkars, the Vishwanathan Anands, the Narayan Murthys and the Warren Buffetts. Given access to such an environment, many more young men and women will prove to be the next generation's Bill Gates, Akio Moritas, Deepak Parekhs and Virender Sehwags.

In this book I have tried to apply this construct to the investment management profession in India. My decade of stockbroking

---

[2] *Bounce: The Myth of Talent and the Power of Practice*, Matthew Syed, (Harper Collins, 2010), pgs 15–16.

experience has allowed me to observe fund managers in two different countries—the UK and India—at close quarters. And what I have seen has convinced me that success in managing large sums of money over long periods of time comes from:

- A decade or so of intense training in analysing companies, quizzing management teams, cultivating primary data sources and understanding the business cycle;
- An almost obsessive focus on intellectual integrity (an avoidance of short cuts in researching, understanding and diligencing a company) even after the initial period of apprenticeship is over to ensure that clients' wealth is preserved and harnessed in an optimal fashion; and
- The ability—created through training, self-awareness and humility—to successfully deal with greed and fear on a daily basis and thereby peel away from other investors who succumb to these primal emotions.

Just as interesting, are the behaviourial traits that are NOT demonstrated by successful fund managers. Making a great deal of money over long periods of time in the stock market:

- Has very little to do with greed or with wanting to be super rich. In fact, paradoxical as it may sound, avarice seems to be a deeply destructive trait in the stock market.
- Relies as much on knowledge of politics, of psychology and of culture as it does on financial knowledge. In fact, the best fund managers tend to be deeply inquisitive and curious individuals who are as interested in, say, the 1971 India-Pakistan War or the reasons for India's decline in Test Cricket as they are in the latest P/E (Price/Earnings) multiple of the Sensex.
- Has very little to do with aggression, personality projection and the sort of behaviour you see in Hollywood movies which have Wall Street as its central subject. The gurus described in this book like to maintain a low profile. Whilst none of them can be called introverts, very few of them are media personalities.

The core point of this book is not that you and I can or can't become superstar fund managers. Our ability to do so is no greater or lesser than our ability to become chess grandmasters or award winning authors or celebrity chefs, but to achieve that level of proficiency we need to put in the sort of intense effort over extended periods of time that the men described in this book have put in.

As the legendary British fund manager, Anthony Bolton, wrote after his retirement, 'Experience is valuable. As Mark Twain put it, "history never repeats itself but it rhymes"—the same patterns do re-occur over time and one is not a seasoned investor until one has experienced a full economic and stock market cycle.'[3]

In this regard, the grind required to become a successful long-term investor is similar to the journey that most successful novelists follow. There is no short cut to accumulating the many layers of experience, knowledge and perspective which a decade on the coal face of the stock market gives you. But time alone is not enough. Quintessentially middle class character traits—such as a strong work ethic, humility, curiosity—combined with independence of mind and character are central to success.

Ten years ago, when I started out as an equity analyst in a firm that I co-founded with a few other analysts, I remember calling British fund managers with small cap investment ideas from our cramped offices in a small flat in south London. To my surprise I found that most of the legends of UK small cap investing were happy to spend time on the phone discussing ideas with me. Even as I sweated my way through my 'learner's license' in equity research, I received a call in February 2004 from a gentleman called David Ross of Aberforth Partners, an Edinburgh based investment house. Even though I was a novice, I knew that Aberforth Partners was the premier small cap investment house in the UK and managed several billion pounds from a town house in Edinburgh. David Ross, a Partner in the firm, was a reputed high priest in the art of 'value investing'.

Fund managers rarely call brokers—that's a fact of life a broker comes to term with very early in his career. So for a rookie like me, David Ross calling was like Sachin Tendulkar calling a schoolboy cricketer. My excitement turned into panic as David said that

---

[3] *Investing Against the Tide*, Anthony Bolton, (FT Prentice Hall, 2009), pg 157.

'I have been reading your research. I would like to come and meet you in your offices.' Horrified at the thought of a legendary investor visiting our office-in-a-flat in the wrong part of London, I tried every trick in the book to convince David that his visit was unnecessary. After all, I said, I was happy to jump on the first flight to Edinburgh and sprint from the airport towards Aberforth's offices on Melville Street. David was having none of it. He clearly wanted to see who we were and what our offices were like. So, reluctantly, I gave him our address.

Finally, the big day arrived—it was as if the Pope himself was visiting. The small team smartened itself up and waited for the door bell to ring. David arrived, had his first mug of coffee and then said that he had understood from the freshness of our work that we were a start-up. He had come to encourage us to step-up our efforts, to assure us that his firm would pay for our work and, most importantly, to guide us through the tricky waters of small cap investing. He did not need to come; we were happy to go to Scotland to meet him. He came because he was curious, he wanted to meet the new kids on the block in their backyard and to encourage a team which he felt could help uncover fresh investment ideas in the years to come.

This counterintuitive pattern of behaviour—that the most successful long-term investors are often those who are most open to meeting new people, most willing to hear new ideas and most open to spending hours discussing the art of investing—is symptomatic of what makes these individuals stand out.

WHY FOCUS ON LONG-TERM INVESTORS?

Before we dive into the structure of the book, I should explain why I have focused on successful long-term investors in this book as opposed to, say, short-term speculators. Whilst there are other successful modes of investing in equity market, their ability to deliver sustained market outperformance over long periods of time, (say, three years or more) is unproven in the Indian context. In more mature markets, such as the US, which have much greater liquidity and greater transparency, short term trading can be and has been successfully practiced over long periods of time by legendary American investors such as George Soros, Julian Robertson and Michael Steinhardt.

However, given that India is the least liquid amongst the world's fifteen largest equity markets, the only viable option open to those who want to deploy large sums of capital successfully is long-term investing. Hence this book focuses on how some of the most successful long-term investors in India have trained their minds relentlessly over the last twenty years so as to be able to consistently outperform the index.

In the ensuing chapters of this book, we delve into the three critical aspects which characterise successful long-term investing:
• Relentless research;
• Simple thumb rules for successful investing; and
• Patience, character and contrarianism.

The final chapter of the book then uses the latest research in neuroscience and psychology and focuses on the question of 'Can you become a successful long-term investor?'

These chapters are interspersed by interviews with some of the gurus who have succeeded in the Indian market for a decade or more. The interviews with these legends are meant to illustrate in practical terms the concepts highlighted in the chapters.

Immediately after this chapter we speak to Sanjoy Bhattacharya. As mentioned before, Sanjoy was instrumental in building the powerhouse that HDFC Asset Management is today. After *Chapter 2* we interview Alroy Lobo who, like Sanjoy, after a distinguished career as an equity analyst, took charge of the asset management business of Kotak Mahindra Bank. Under Alroy's stewardship, over the past seven years Kotak has become one of the top ten mutual fund houses in India. After *Chapter 3*, we meet two unique investors: Akash Prakash, one of the first high profile fund managers in India to set up his own fund management house (Amansa), and Sankaran Naren, the CIO of ICICI Prudential Mutual Fund. Naren is the only Indian CIO known to me who started investing his father's money even whilst he was in high school in Chennai. By the time, Naren joined ICICI Prudential as a fund manager in 2004, he had been investing in the stock market for nearly 15 years.

Over the past decade, First State Stewart, part of First State Investments, has emerged as one of the biggest foreign institutional investors not only in the Indian market but, more generally, across emerging markets. In a world where many consider financial markets to be a playground for greedy, unprincipled men, First State Stewart's rise comes as a pleasant surprise for it has been based on focusing heavily on investing in businesses which are run by ethical management teams which keep the interests of all stakeholders—not just shareholders but also employees and the wider community—in mind. Sashi Reddy, one of First State Stewart's fund managers, shares his thoughts after *Chapter 4*.

Finally, after *Chapter 5* we meet two investors who, in parallel with Sanjoy Bhattacharya, played a pioneering role in establishing the commercial credentials of long-term investing in India. BN Manjunath is one of the very first professional fund managers in India. Manjunath started investing in stocks in the dark days of the 'license Raj' as part of the Treasury team of a public sector bank. His journey from the bowels of Canara Bank to being the trusted advisor for one of the most successful hedge funds in Asia, Ward Ferry, is worthy of being captured on celluloid. The final interview in this book is of a fund manager who has recently retired but who, when he was in active service, was managing half of my modest net worth as the CIO of an iconic fund management house. 'Anonymous', as I have had to call him given that his erstwhile employer is publicity shy, is perhaps the only man that some of the other investors who were interviewed for this book would gladly give their money to if they had to choose someone else to manage their wealth.

The book has been written such that it can be read, both, as a linear narrative which goes through the chapters and the interviews as they are laid out or as a collection of interviews for those who are already familiar with the basic tenets of fundamentally oriented equity investing.

'MY INVESTMENT PHILOSOPHY IS VERY OLD FASHIONED'

Sanjoy Bhattacharyya *is currently the Principal Adviser to Oceandial, an investment management boutique. He was the founding CIO of HDFC Asset Management, India's largest mutual fund. Sanjoy is the guru, mentor and friend to several of the country's leading investors and analysts. Educated at Mayo College (Ajmer), Loyola College (Chennai) and IIM (Ahmedabad), Sanjoy is also passionate about contract bridge and aims to play competitive bridge at the highest level.*

Before we go on to discuss your investment philosophy could you give us a sense of what shaped it?

SB: That came about when I first started reading about investment in the late 1980s. I read all sorts of stuff to begin with. I started off by reading Graham & Dodd's *Security Analyst* because my day job at that time was that of a credit rating analyst. And yet I did not know the ABC of analysing balance sheets or how to look at businesses. That ignorance in turn stemmed from the fact that during my MBA I majored in Marketing; I did not do a single course in Finance. And there was an irony in that—I did not want to follow in my father's footsteps (my father was among the best known professors in Accounting and Finance in the country).

In order to reject following your father's footsteps you chose Marketing. Then how did you enter the field of Finance?

SB: Because I realised Marketing is not for me, I tried it for five years but ultimately came to the conclusion that I did not have the mindset. The other choice I had was to join my dad in the management consulting practice he had created. My dad was probably the first Asian professor at Harvard Business School in 1969 when Indians were a fairly rare species in US academia. He was also a visiting faculty member at Stanford. Among others, he was fortunate to work alongside Marvin Bower, the founder of McKinsey.

It was my first introduction to individuals like Purnendu Chatterjee (founder and chairman of The Chatterjee Group) and Rajat Gupta (the now disgraced but formerly celebrated Managing Director of McKinsey) who lived in Boston at the time. CK Prahlad (the celebrated Indian management guru), Srikanth Datar (professor of Accounting at Harvard Business School) and a host of other exceptionally gifted students from IIM Ahmedabad (IIM-A) in the early years were students of my father. Funnily enough, I was admitted to IIM-A by Vijay Govindarajan (a global expert on strategy and innovation) who was then my father's research associate.

In those days the obvious thing to do would have been to migrate. How come you did not migrate?

SB: Vikram Sarabhai recruited a group of academics in 1963, including my father, with the intention of building a world class academic institution. Given the amazing leadership of Prof. Ravi Mathai and the exceptional commitment of the founding group, IIM-A blossomed remarkably during that period. Quite apart from his skill as a teacher, my father also became well known as a strategy consultant by virtue of his exposure to individuals at McKinsey during his stint at HBS. It struck me that if I were to join his consulting practice, there was a high likelihood that I would live in his shadow. Being young, my misplaced sense of idealism led me to abandon such a path! However, there was absolutely no clarity on what made sense. By a process of elimination, I decided to take on a marketing job and keep my options open by applying for admission to a doctoral programme. At worst, that would allow me to eventually join my father's consulting firm.

Whilst I was waiting to go to the US, I met my wife, Indrani, when I was in MARG (a market research firm). I worked there for just over 4 years. That's where I got to see a lot of different companies, particularly consumer-based companies. And I realised that understanding what these companies were doing is fascinating. In the meantime there was a classmate of mine who joined Asian Paints when we graduated from IIM-A in May 1982.

His name is IK Jaiswal (Regional Vice President, International, at Asian Paints) and he is, in a number of ways, like an elder brother. Asian Paints went public in September 1982, a few months after IK joined them. He used to always joke that, 'I work here and if you ever feel like buying shares of a listed company, you should buy Asian Paints' shares because in the end, I am going to make a serious impact.'

Asian Paints went public in September 1982 at a price of ₹27. Within six months, it doubled in price. I bought Asian Paints shares at ₹53 as a token of my respect for IK. I bought these shares with my total savings in the bank which was ₹15,000. As a result, Asian Paints was my first investment but in reality it happened because of IK's ability to keep a dead-pan expression while joking! Then as I watched the shares go up from 1983 onwards I thought to myself that 'this is some kind of miracle' and I wanted to understand how such miracles happen.

You were a marketing professional at that time?

SB: Yes, I thought if I can get a better handle on how companies perform, it might actually give me a chance of becoming seriously rich. Being a professor's son and a middle class Brahmin, I thought there is nothing wrong if I can get rich this way. I couldn't think of any other way of doing it and I thought this is a good way. So from 1983–87 my portfolio was a one share portfolio—Asian Paints. Then I did an incredibly dumb thing. In those days if you sold your shares to buy a house, you did not have to pay Capital Gains Tax (CGT). My initial investment of ₹15,000 in Asian Paints became so big that in 1990 it amounted to ₹6 lakh. At that time, you could buy a house in the suburbs of Mumbai for ₹6 lakh. To save CGT I bought a house near Nallasopara (a town on the outskirts of Mumbai), which was the biggest mistake of my life. If I had held on to the Asian Paints shares, today they would be worth in excess of ₹5 crore. That's what got my interest going in equities. I then read *One Up on Wall Street* by Peter Lynch and *Security Analysis* by Graham & Dodd and trained myself to read a balance sheet. Very few MBAs know the nuances behind reading a financial statement.

Even amongst professional financial analysts, a large number of them could improve their ability to read a balance sheet.

Why do you think that this state of affairs has come about?

SB: If you learn a language you have to do it systematically. You need to learn the alphabet, the structure, the grammar; you need to learn various things whereas most analysts tend to look at things in a disjointed manner. So for them it's not like a language. It does not make sense to them. They know the elements, they know the adjectives, adverbs and nouns but they don't see the flow, they don't see the balance sheet coming together as a whole. I haven't seen too many analysts reading the 'Notes to the accounts' and relating it to the balance sheet.

You read 'Notes to the accounts', you look at the contingent liabilities, you look at the net worth, you look at the extent of borrowing and you can ask yourself 'tomorrow if something happens, what does it do to the company and what is the likelihood of the event having serious negative consequences'. Like in the pharma companies with the DPCO (Drug Pricing Control Order). I used to be scared to invest in Glaxo in the 1990s because I used to be scared about what would happen to Glaxo if this DPCO came through. That was a wrong judgment on my part because the order did not materialise and it hasn't materialised twenty years later but I got scared.

But it was part of your learning experience?

SB: Absolutely. Pradip Shah (Crisil's first Managing Director and Sanjoy's one time boss) gave us phenomenal freedom and I mentioned this in the book called *Money Monarchs* by Chetan Parikh. I acknowledge in that book the role of Pradip Shah in making me a rational and thoughtful analyst. He encouraged us to do everything we could do to investigate companies: 'to investigate without being scared and see and do whatever is necessary so that the opinion is as good as it can be.' He was also a great intellect and perfectly willing to share his skills and insight. Equally, he was instrumental in nurturing a great work ethic. I learned how to read a balance sheet largely because of Mr Shah! I used to read the balance sheet and write notes. Mr Shah would read the notes and ask me 'is this really what the balance sheet says?' Then he would answer his own question and tell me what the balance sheet really said.

He asked me once, 'Banks take working capital as collateral and because this loan has collateral against it, you are saying that this bank is very well protected. So let's assume that tomorrow this borrower defaults, is the bank safe? Can the bank actually sell inventory of semi-finished steel products? Who will be the buyer for such products? There is no liquid market for these products. The fact it is valued on the balance sheet at such-and-such price does not mean that the bank is safe.'

Mr Shah also taught us that 'when you lend money it's not the collateral that matters, it is the earning power of the company. At the end of the day it is the earning power that is the important element in determining credit quality, it is not how much collateral you have. You can have any amount of collateral and still have serious trouble.' Unfortunately, the whole Indian banking system runs on collateral. Very few Indians understand this point. Pradip Shah used to go into the details. I remember going with him to see a famous industrialist in Pune. I was the leader of the team for that rating. He said, 'Sanjoy, I will catch up with you tomorrow morning at the Taj Blue Diamond. We will meet at the coffee shop at 8:30am and have breakfast. By 9:30am we have to be at the industrialist's office. So you can brief me in 5–10 minutes.' When we met in the morning I told him that there are four elements to focus on: there is capital employed, this is the history of profitability, this is how operating margins have progressed, they have competition from so-and-so, this is where this company has a technology problem. I thought I had mastered the show. I was waiting for the applause at the end of my monologue. As I concluded, Mr Shah enquired about the idiosyncrasies of a particular family member. Needless to add, my homework was inadequate but it instilled in me an abiding passion for detail. The other lesson was that character counts just as much as debt servicing ability in arriving at a credit opinion. So knowing about the habits of family members in the sponsor group can have a great deal of relevance to the willingness of a company to meet its obligations. It is precisely because of these reasons that I was blessed to work for CRISIL. Finally, I got the education that had passed me by earlier. Here is another quaint illustration of trivia that matters. Do you know how Cummins came to India? *(Cummins, an American company, is a leading manufacturer of generators.)*

Kirloskar brothers had brought them to India I presume.
SB: Not quite. Shantanu Kirloskar studied at MIT and he was the roommate of a guy who went on to join Cummins in the US. twenty five years later that guy became the Senior Vice President of the International Business of Cummins. They were in touch and he said, 'I want to come to India' and Kirloskar said that his family would join hands with him. That is how Kirloskar Cummins was established.

Not only because they had immense integrity...

SB: But because they used to share the same room at MIT.

You see Pradip Shah's role in your life in a similar vein?

SB: Yes, that was great training and then there was my father. He was not a formal mentor but he taught me in a way that I think is the best way to learn. He just kept on pointing out my mistakes. He would tell me 'Are you serious? Do you really think you should invest in this company?' His view on the stock market until a few years before his death was that it was a gambling den. Until that point he did not invest at all in the market. In the last five years of this life, 1988–93, he invested in the market. Had he been alive he would have been one of the 5–6 best investors in the country. He really had an incredible understanding of the Indian business. He made predictions which are not related to investment but for the management columns that he wrote for *Business India* in the early years when it was set up in the 1970s. There is a *Business India* cover story which I still have in its original form. The cover page illustration has a weighing scale. On one side of the scale are the MNCs. On the other side are pictures of Dhirubhai Ambani, Karsanbhai Patel and Brijmohan Lal Munjal. My father wrote the centerpiece for that issue and he said that Indian industry will come into its own. Remember, this was way back in 1978. Dhirubhai was relatively unknown at that time; his firm was called Reliance Textile Industries. Brijmohan Munjal hadn't even set up Hero Honda; he was still manufacturing Hero cycles.

My father's understanding of business was based on his life as a civil servant, a professor and a consultant. So he had a tremendous understanding of how the government works and the linkage between government and business. Which is why I suspect Vikram Sarabhai recruited him for IIM-A. He felt that someone should be there who should understand government and what business means to government.

After Crisil you moved to ICRA and then stock-broking?

SB: In between, when my father passed away I joined Morgan Stanley Asset Management as a consultant. That is the time I met Akash Prakash (subsequently the founder of Amansa) and helped him with stock selection for the Morgan Stanley Growth Fund. In a sense, it was time to pass on the benefits of my experience at Crisil. After Morgan Stanley, I moved to SG Warburg.

How long were you there?

SB: Four and a half years. I learnt that the distinction between the buy-side and the sell-side is artificial. Equally, while research on the sell-side may have great sophistication most of the time it lacks intellectual integrity. I also learnt a lot of things about the great British firm SG Warburg...the way they think, their approach. I think that was central to what made them special. The minute it became Swiss, it got diluted.

The single biggest thing that hit me was the importance of written communication and my failings in this regard. In Warburg, everyone was from either Cambridge, the London School of Economics or from Oxford. There was no room for lesser mortals!

At Warburg, when you went to a meeting in the City of London, the junior most guy had to come back to office and write up the meeting notes. I was always that guy when I worked in London with Warburg. So I used to write the note and you are not allowed to write pages and pages of it. The note had to be brief and deal with all that mattered because it would go the big bosses. So I wrote a note after we had met with a large Indian company passing through London. My boss read it and said, 'Well done, Sanjoy'. I looked at him knowing something was amiss. My boss said, 'But you clearly haven't heard of a thing called the split infinitive, have you?' I learned the craft of writing in a precise manner at SG Warburg! Clearly, my education was a work in progress. I also learned the need for discipline, the need for making notes at the end of the day and many other things that were just the state of the art at that time. For example, the concept of Enterprise Value and the idea behind thematic research. Warburg wrote copious notes on equity research which had little to do with companies, notes which were entirely theme driven. I learnt about many concepts simply because I was there at Warburg and they would do very good industry related work.

Warburg took you around the world. Was that experience useful?

SB: Yes, incredibly so. I got a first-hand exposure to the difference in attitudes between fund managers in Europe, America and Asia.

Did that influence your investing philosophy?

SB: My investing philosophy is very old fashioned and greatly influenced by Ben Graham's emphasis on a margin of safety. More recently, I have been drawn to the Joel Greenblatt approach (magic formula investing) which attempts to buy sustainable earning power as cheap as possible. The truly important lessons that I have learnt in the last couple of decades with regard to investing are above all stay patient, have true humility and always retain the zest to develop intellectually. The need to have an eclectic mindset, read extensively and have a genuinely multi-disciplinary perspective is absolutely vital. It is probably far more important to study psychology, statistics and sociology than economics and accounting! A number of people believe that since India is a relatively high growth economy, 'growth' investing is the mantra for India. I am not so sure that the answer is as obvious as that. Rational capital allocation and the ability of management to build trust across a range of constituents including customers, regulators and investors matter significantly to the long-term investor in India.

If one considers market structure, putting aside the 200 largest stocks by market caps, the next 800 or so stocks are poorly researched by investors in spite of the fact that financial information on these companies is now relatively easy to access. The 'neglect' of these stocks gives investors fertile grounds for profit. Secondly, whilst India is morphing from an utterly momentum driven market to one where fundamentals are playing a greater role, information dissemination and stock-specific analysis is still less than 'efficient' in India. That in turn creates opportunities for investors who are willing to conduct extensive fundamental analysis. Thirdly, whilst I would like to believe that the 'Growth at a reasonable price' (GARP) approach works in India in most situations, it is clear that no one approach works in India all the time. In fact, over the long-term, value investing works in India to a greater extent than in most other markets.

For example, 'value investing' led us to Infosys in the early 1990s when I was at Morgan Stanley. We bought it because it was dirt cheap relative to cash-flow, relative to earnings, relative to the quality of the people who were running it.

How do you maintain 'selling discipline'?

SB: With great difficulty (laughing)! Selling is well and truly the dark continent of investing. I get too worked up about short-term changes in competitive pressure, about losses in market share. For example, I sold Glaxo SmithKline Consumer, a large personal holding, way too early in the 1990s as I was worried that Cadbury's entry into the 'white' market would hurt Horlicks. Cadbury launched the new product at bargain basement prices which rattled me into believing that it would blow Glaxo away. Based on that knee jerk premise I sold, which was a gigantic mistake. Great companies can survive sporadic upsurges in competition. Survivorship is one of the tests of high quality companies but I did not realise that then.

The three rules that I tend to use are: (a) Sell when you see a clear reduction in the quality or strength of the franchise and hence a reduction in its earning power; (b) Sell when the stock price exceeds your estimate of fair value by a considerable amount; (c) Sell when the assumptions that you made vis a vis the stock or the catalysts that you expected turn out to be unrealistic.

All of that being said, I still struggle to sell well and often have to use an even simpler selling rule: Sell when the value of a recent investment falls by 15 per cent or more.

How did you end up becoming the first CIO of HDFC Asset Management?

SB: To this day, that question remains a complete mystery to me. Deepak Parekh, for reasons I still cannot fathom, plucked me from obscurity to be the CIO of HDFC Asset Management. I left Warburg in December 1998 after UBS merged with Warburg. Since working at Warburg helped me achieve a sense of financial freedom, I chose to manage my own money and that of a friend after leaving UBS. The fact that I owned a number of IT companies in a fairly sizeable way made it look all too easy. I felt the time had come to hone my skills as a bridge player. Sadly, that was not to be. One morning my mother walked into office and was aghast to see me playing bridge on the computer. In a fairly matter of fact way, she said 'this is simply not on, you are wasting your life.' On leaving Warburg, I went and met Mr Parekh in early 1999. I remember saying that 'Sir, if ever you set up an asset management firm, I would be happy to work in any capacity that you think fit. I would just be delighted to be a part of it'. Suddenly one day in January 2000, I got a call from one of his secretaries. The rest, as they say, is history.

I don't think it has ever happened ever before or since in Indian investment management that a guy with absolutely no prior experience in investment management has been catapulted to his level of incompetence at the first shot. Quite obviously my selection as CIO of HDFC Asset Management was not a reflection of my capability as an experienced investment hand. More likely, it was a reflection of the faith that Mr Parekh had in the cultural fit and my desire to keep it simple and stay honest. He knew my father for many years. That probably worked in my favour in terms of his being able to trust me. The sense of fiduciary responsibility that HDFC Asset Management inculcated in me is one of the lessons that I truly cherish.

TWO

Relentless Research

'What distinguishes investment winners, as you'll see in this book, is the willingness to dig deeper, search more widely and keep an open mind to all ideas—including the idea that you might have made a bad call. He or she who turns over the most rocks, looks over the most investment ideas, and is unsentimental about past choices is most likely to succeed.'— Peter Lynch, writing in the foreword to Anthony Bolton's *Investing Against the Tide*[1]

THE LONG ROAD TO INVESTMENT SUCCESS

The American investor-cum-author, John Train, paints a riveting portrait of former Fidelity legend Peter Lynch, who retired in 1992 with his Magellan fund standing at over US$12 bn of AUM or assets under management (compared to the mere US$22 million invested in it when he took charge in 1977 having spent, at that point, eight years in Fidelity as an analyst). Train points out that Lynch's work

---

[1] Foreword, *Investing Against the Tide*, Anthony Bolton, (FT Prentice Hall, 2009), pg xiv.

day began at 6.15am (reading annual reports and research carried out by broking firms on his way to work) and ended at 7.15pm (still reading annual reports and financial research as Fidelity's company bus dropped him home). This legendary fund manager worked Saturdays as a matter of course and did not take a single vacation in the fifteen years he ran Magellan.[2]

Even more extraordinarily, Peter Lynch travelled around 10,000 miles a year (that's 40 miles every day) in order to meet companies. In fact, he met 40 or 50 companies per month, almost two companies each day. He prepared thoroughly for each meeting; spending nearly two hours reading all available material on the company. When you put it all together, a picture emerges of a packed daily calendar of travel, meetings (where Lynch took meticulous notes), researching and, most importantly, buying and selling stocks worth hundreds of millions of dollars. (Train says that roughly one in ten companies that Lynch met impressed him enough for him to put money to work.)

Writing a decade or so before Malcolm Gladwell, Matthew Syed and others popularised the idea of '10,000 hours of practice' being required to attain mastery in a specific discipline, John Train echoed their thinking when he wrote: '...dedication right from one's youth is what it takes for greatness in any field; to win an Olympic gold medal in gymnastics, to beat the Russians at chess, to star in the New York City Ballet. And Lynch is in that league. Great success, alas, usually requires obsession. Differently put, you won't get there if you don't love it so much that you'd rather do it than anything else, whether or not it's worth that dedication. As an ancient French saying has it, La joie de l'esprit en fait la force—loosely translated, "The spirit's joy gives it power." Delight in his craft is Lynch's secret.'[3]

As a broker I get to see Indian fund managers go through exactly this journey. And when I take a company's CEO to meet fund managers, I can see that investors vary in how extensively they prepare for their meetings with corporates. Watching an

---

[2] Chapter 17, *Money Masters of Our Time*, John Train, (HarperCollins, 2003).

[3] *Money Masters of Our Time*, John Train, (HarperCollins, 2003), pg 298.

experienced and well prepared fund manager probe a seasoned Indian promoter, I often ask myself: 'How on earth did the investor think of that question?' or 'Why did I not think of that unique perspective on this firm?' And therein lies the secret to generating insights from research—all professional investors broadly have the same information set—financial statements, broker research, meetings with management and access to industry experts—and yet only a select few use the information to ask the question unasked by others and see the perspective hidden to most.

In this chapter we will delve into the core functional strength of an astute investor: researching a broad swathe of companies, relentlessly and systematically year after year. We will examine the four broad areas that professional investors focus their research efforts on:

1. The strength of the franchise;
2. The quality of the financial statements;
3. The promoter's competence; and
4. The promoter's integrity.

THE STRENGTH OF THE FRANCHISE

The first thing a fundamentally oriented long term investor asks is 'Does this company have sustainable competitive advantages which gives it an edge over its rivals?' Amongst the great investors of our time, Warren Buffet has captured this concept most memorably using the metaphor of 'competitive moats'.

'I don't want an easy business for competitors. I want a business with a moat around it. I want a very valuable castle in the middle and I want the duke who is in charge of that castle to be very honest and hardworking and able. Then I want a moat around that castle. The moat can be various things. The moat around our auto insurance business, GEICO, is low cost.'[4]

---

[4] Lecture by Warren Buffett at the University of Florida's School of Business, 15 October 1998.

Whilst the phrase 'competitive advantage' has now become part of the daily financial lexicon, it is worth understanding what it means in the context of investment analysis.

Since all firms use a collection of inputs to generate a certain output, the difference between inputs and output can be called 'value addition'. Obviously, the more additional value a firm generates, the more successful it will be. So, why do we find, within the same industry, some firms doing better on this score than others? The answer lies in 'competitive advantage'; competitive advantage is what helps a certain firm add more value than its rivals. Why is it that certain firms seem to have more competitive advantage than others? In his 1993 book, *Foundations of Corporate Success*, John Kay, the British economist and *Financial Times* columnist, has written more comprehensibly and clearly about this than any other business guru.[5] (A quick confession here: After graduating from the London School of Economics, I was fortunate enough to work with John, first, in the firm that he co-founded, London Economics, and then in the firm that I co-founded in the UK, Clear Capital, where John was the Chairman. A lot of what I practice today and what I have written here is the direct result of John's influence.)

John says that 'sustainable competitive advantage' is what helps a firm ensure that the value that it adds cannot be competed away by its rivals. It can come from two sources: distinctive capabilities or strategic assets. Whilst strategic assets can be in the form of intellectual property (patents, proprietary knowhow), or legal rights (licenses, concessions) or in the form a natural monopoly, distinctive capabilities are more intangible in nature.

Distinctive capabilities, says Kay, are the relationships that a firm has with its customers, suppliers or employees which cannot be replicated by other competing firms and which allow the firm to add more value than its competitors. He further divides distinctive capabilities into three categories:

---

[5] Part III, *Foundations of Corporate Success*, John Kay, (Oxford University Press, 1993).

- Brands and reputation
- Architecture
- Innovation

Let us delve into the capabilities in more detail as one needs to understand these to comprehend the strength of a company's franchise.

Brands and reputation

In a number of markets, product quality, in spite of being an important driver of the purchase decision, can only be ascertained by long term experience of using that product. Examples of such products are insurance policies and healthcare. In many other markets, the ticket price of the product is high; hence the consumer is able to assess the quality of the product only after he has parted with his cash. Examples would be cars and high-end television sets.

In both of these markets, customers use the strength of the company's reputation as a proxy for the quality of the product or the service. For example, we gravitate towards the best hospital in town for critical surgery and we tend to prefer world class brands whilst buying expensive home entertainment equipment. Since reputations for such products take years, is difficult and costly to build, it becomes a powerful source of competitive advantage.

In products that we use on a daily basis, we are generally aware of the strength of a brand. However in niche or in (business to business) B2B product segments (e.g. industrial cables, mining equipment, municipal water purification, semiconductors), investors often do not have first hand knowledge of the key brands in the relevant market. To assess the strength of the brand, investors turn to:

- Brand recognition surveys conducted by the trade press,
- The length of the warranties offered by the firm (the longer the warranties, the more unequivocal the statement it makes about the firm's brand),
- The amount of time the firm has been in that market (e.g. 'Established 1905' is a fairly credible way of telling the world

that since you have been in business for over a century, your product must have something distinctive about it),

- How much the firm spends on its marketing and publicity (a large marketing spend figure, relative to the firm's revenues, is usually a reassuring sign), and
- How much of a price premium the firm is able to charge vis a vis its peers.

One way to appreciate the power of brands and reputation to generate sustained profits and hence, shareholder returns, is to look at how India's most trusted brands, have fared over the last decade. An analysis done by the financial daily, *Economic Times*, which can be seen in the table below, shows that over the past decade the listed companies with the most powerful brands have

TABLE 1.1

#	Company	Trusted Brands*	10 Year Growth (FY04–14) (%CAGR)**		
			Revenues	EPS	Share price
1	Colgate-Palmolive	Colgate (1)	14	17	27
2	Hindustan Unilever	Clinic Plus (4), Lifebuoy (10), Rin (12), Surf (13), Lux (14, Ponds, etc	10	8	15
3	Nestle	Maggi (9), Nestle Milk Chocolate (62), etc	15	16	23
4	GSK Consumer	Horlicks (16)	15	21	33
5	Bharti Airtel	Airtel (18)	33	18	15
	Average for the listed companies with the top 5 brands		18	16	22
	Average for the Nifty companies		12	13	14

Source: Economic Times and Ambit Capital analysis using Bloomberg data.
* Figures in brackets indicate rank in the 2012 Economic Times 'brand equity' survey to find the 100 most trusted brands in India. ** The FY14 data is based on Bloomberg consensus as on 7 April 2014.

comfortably beaten the most widely acknowledged frontline stock market index by a comfortable margin on revenues, earnings and share price movement.[6]

Architecture

'Architecture' refers to the network of contracts, formal and informal, that a firm has with its employees, suppliers and customers. It would include the formal employment contracts that a firm has with its employees and the more informal obligation it has to provide ongoing training to its employees. Similarly, architecture would include the firm's legal obligation to pay its suppliers on time and its more informal obligation to warn its suppliers in advance if it were planning to cut production in three months' time.

Such architecture is most often found in firms with a distinctive organisational style or ethos as such firms tend to have a well organised and long established set of processes or routines for doing business. So, for example, if you have ever taken a home loan in India, you will find a marked difference in the speed and professionalism with which HDFC processes a home loan application compared to other lenders. The HDFC branch manager asks the applicant more specific questions than other lenders do and this home loan provider's due diligence on the applicant and the property seems to be done more swiftly and thoroughly than most other lenders in India.

Another example of architecture can be seen in the suburb of Mumbai where I live, Hiranandani Gardens in Powai. In the mid-1980s, the Hiranandani family sold their first tranche of flats in what was then a far flung suburb on Mumbai, quite literally in the middle of a forest. Even in the early 1990s, taxi drivers were reluctant to ferry passengers to Hiranandani Gardens because the remoteness of the region and the abundant forest cover made this an ideal location for highway robbers to ply their trade.

---

[6] *The Economic Times*, 7 November, 2012.

However, over the last 20 years, Hiranandani Developers has gradually built a network of institutions in the area—a large school, a well-equipped hospital, a well-stocked supermarket, two hotels (budget and luxury), a thriving high street with several good restaurants, many banks, a variety of stores selling general provisions and two neighbourhood shopping malls. The developer also sponsors a range of other initiatives in the area such as an annual marathon, cultural festivals and several local clubs. By offering an ever expanding network of services beyond the standard amenities (eg. parks, swimming pools, decent roads), Hiranandani Gardens has become a sought after residential area. This 'architecture' allows this family owned real estate developer to now charge rates for new flats which are double that charged by any other developer in this part of Mumbai. Since the cost of building residential real estate is broadly the same for the Hiranandani family as it is for other developers in suburban Mumbai (all of them got hold of their land banks more than a decade or so ago through controversial means), the profit margins that Hiranandani Developers generates is likely to be significantly higher than those earned by most other developers in Mumbai.

So how can an investor assess whether the firm under scrutiny has requisite architecture? It is a difficult task but an investor can gauge whether a firm has such processes and procedures by examining the:

- Extent to which the employees of the firm co-operate with each other across various departments and locations,
- The rate of staff attrition (sometimes given in the annual report),
- Extent to which staff in different parts of the firm give the same message when asked the same question, and
- Extent to which the firm is able to generate innovations in its products or services or production processes on an ongoing basis.

At the core of successful architecture is co-operation—co-operation within teams, across various teams in a firm and between a firm and its suppliers—and sharing—sharing of ideas, information, customer insights and, ultimately, rewards.

Built properly, architecture allows a firm with ordinary people to produce extraordinary results. Perhaps the most striking demonstration of architecture in India is the unlisted non-profit agricultural co-operative, Gujarat Cooperative Milk Marketing Federation Ltd (GCMMF), better known to millions of Indians as 'Amul'.

With its roots stretching back to India's freedom movement, GCMMF was founded by the legendary Verghese Kurien in 1973. This farmer's co-operative generated revenues of ₹137 billion (around US$2.1 billon) in FY13 thus making it significantly bigger than its main private sector competitor, Nestle (FY13 revenues of ₹91 billion or around US$1.5 billon). Furthermore, GCMMF's revenues have grown by 21 per cent per annum over the past five years as opposed to Nestle's 16 per cent per annum over the same period.

GCMMF's daily milk procurement of 13 million litres from over 16,000 village milk co-operative societies (which include 3.2 million milk producer members) has become the stuff of legend. The way GCMMF aggregates the milk produced by over 3 million families into the village co-operative dairy and then further aggregates that into the district co-operative which in turn feeds into the mother dairy has been studied by numerous management experts.

Not only does GCMMF possess impressive logistical skills, its marketing acumen is comparable to that of many multinational giants. In key FMCG product categories such as butter, cheese and packaged milk, Amul has been the longstanding market leader in the face of sustained efforts by global conglomerates to break its dominance. GCMMF is also India's biggest exporter of dairy products.

How does GCMMF do it? How does it give a fair deal to farmers, its management team (which includes the alumnus from India's best business schools), its 5,000 dealers, its one million retailers and its hundreds of millions of customers? Numerous case studies have been written on GCMMF, but at the core of this co-operative's success appear to be three factors: (a) its 50 year old brand with its distinctive imagery of the little girl in the polka red dotted dress; (b) the idea of a fair deal for the small farmer and the linked idea of the disintermediation of the unfair middle man; and (c) the sprit of Indian nationalism in an industry dominated by globe girdling for-profit corporates.

Innovation

Innovation is often talked about as a source of competitive advantage, especially in the technology and pharmaceutical sectors. However those who have studied the phenomenon closely would back me up when I say that it is actually the most tenuous source of sustainable competitive advantage. Innovation is:

- Expensive,
- Uncertain—the innovation process tends to be 'hit or miss',
- Hard to manage due to the random nature of the process.

Furthermore, even when the expensive innovation process yields a commercially useful result, competitors can gnaw away at the benefits by replicating the innovation, and/or employees who have driven the innovation process can seek to extract the benefits of innovation through higher compensation. In fact, innovation is more powerful when it is twinned with the two other distinctive capabilities we have described above—reputation and architecture. Apple is the most celebrated example of a contemporary firm which has clearly built a reputation for innovation.

Strategic Assets

In contrast to the three distinctive capabilities discussed above, strategic assets are easier to identify as sources of competitive advantage. Such assets can come in different guises:

- Intellectual property i.e. patents or proprietary knowhow (e.g. the recipe for Coke's famous syrup which is a closely held secret and kept in the company's museum in Atlanta, Georgia);
- Licenses and regulatory permissions to provide a certain service to the public (e.g. telecom, power, gas or public transport);

- Access to natural resources such as coal or iron-ore mines;
- Political contacts either at the national, state or city level;
- Sunk costs incurred by the first mover which result in other potential competitors deciding to stay away from that market, e.g. given that there already is a Mumbai-Pune highway operated by IRB, it does not make sense for anyone else to set up a competing road;
- Natural monopolies i.e. sectors or markets which accommodate only one or two firms, e.g. the market for supplying power in Mumbai is restricted to one firm—Tata Power.

The firm that owns strategic assets, in whatever form and shape they may be, benefits from lower per unit costs of production relative to its competitors. For example, Tata Steel, on account of its decades-old access to coal and iron-ore from its captive mines, is able to generate more money per ton of steel produced than any other steel manufacturer in the country. According to Ambit Capital's analysts, per ton of steel produced, Tata Steel earns ₹45,000. This compares to ₹39,000 for SAIL and ₹38,000 for JSW Steel.

Unsurprisingly therefore when you look at the top 50 companies by market cap in India since the Nifty was launched in 1995, you find that there is only one conglomerate—Tata Sons that has had three companies which have been in the index more or less throughout this period (Tata Power, Tata Steel and Tata Motors). In fact, as I write this book in the early months of 2014 I find that with four entries—the three firms named in the preceding sentence plus Tata Consultancy Services—Tata Sons beats every other Indian conglomerate hands down in terms of the extent of its presence in the Nifty.

Upon closer examination the Tata group, without being the most innovative player in town, turns out to be an almost text book study of how to build businesses which, combine architecture and brands to great effect thereby creating robust sources of sustainable competitive advantage. The group seems to have created at least three specific mechanisms to ensure that these sources of competitive advantage endure:

Firstly, Tata Sons, an unlisted company (owned by several philanthropic trusts endowed by members of the Tata family), is the promoter of the major operating Tata companies and holds significant shareholdings in these companies. Tata Sons' patient, long term orientation in terms of building large, robust businesses gradually has played a major role in the stability of the listed Tata businesses.

Secondly, Tata Quality Management Services (TQMS), a division of Tata Sons, assists Tata companies in their business excellence initiatives through the Tata Business Excellence Model, Management of Business Ethics and the Tata Code of Conduct.[7] TQMS, quite literally, provides the architecture to harmonise practices in various parts of the Tata empire.

Thirdly, Tata Sons is also the owner of the Tata name and several Tata trademarks, which are registered in India and around the world. These are used by various Tata companies under a licence from Tata Sons as part of their corporate name and/or in relation to their products and services. The terms of use of the group mark and logo by Tata companies are governed by the Brand Equity and Business Promotion Agreement, entered into between Tata Sons and Tata companies.[8]

The primacy of primary data

'I always try and spend the last few minutes...to touch on a competitor, or a company they do business with, such as a supplier or a customer. Although not all managements will talk about other companies, when they do it can be very revealing. The ultimate commendation is when a company talks positively about a competitor. I always put a strong weight on such a view.'—Anthony Bolton, the legendary manager of the Fidelity Special Situations fund[9]

There is no use just speaking to the managing director or

---

[7] The Tata Sons' website.

[8] The Tata Sons' website.

[9] *Investing Against the Tide*, Anthony Bolton, (FT Prentice Hall, 2009), pg 16.

the finance director. You have to be there in the public hall of the SBU where you might meet some of the programmers. I try to do that. I try to go on the field and get a feel of what is happening....I think essentially you always need to have some feeling other than what the management is giving you. That is very important. I think that if a person is not careful and if you are only relying on the views of the management, it can be totally wrong. I think there have to be a lot of other sources and it cannot be just annual reports alone.'—Sukumar Rajah, Managing Director and CIO for Asian Equities at Franklin Templeton Investments[10]

Understanding 'sustainable competitive advantage' as a concept is one thing but, it can be very tricky to establish whether a large, well known company actually possesses sustainable competitive advantages. The company management is unlikely to offer an unbiased view on the subject and since most brokers are clueless about such issues, credible sources of information can only be found in the industry in question. So the relevant company's customers, competitors, suppliers, ex-employees, regulators, former advisors or consultants are often the best sources of information.

Skilled investors know how to seek out such sources (called 'primary data sources' in industry jargon) and ask questions such as:

- Which player is 'price leader' in this market? Or which company raises prices first?
- Which firm is the most desirable employer in this sector? Or which company has the lowest staff attrition rate in the sector?
- Which company has the strongest regulatory and political connections in the sector?
- Which company has best after sales service in this market?
- Which company has the best track record of signing-up new distributors (or new franchises) in this sector? Or which

---

[10] *India's Money Monarchs*, Chetan Parikh, (Capitalideasonline.com, 2005), pg 205.

company has the longest queue of applicants who would like to be distributors (or franchisees)?

Financial analysis to assess competitive advantages

The other method, complementary to the probing method described above, is to use financial ratio analysis to assess whether a company has sustainable competitive advantages. A company with such advantages should have stable or rising operating margins over a ten-year period combined with double digit revenue growth. Such growth in profitability should mean that in spite of investment in plant, capacity, brands, etc, the company has been able to maintain healthy levels of ROCE and ROE (both of these should be at least in the high teens over the ten year period in question). In the next chapter we will look at why this combination of simple rules is such a powerful recipe for sustained corporate success.

Case study: Asian Paints[11]

Asian Paints was founded in 1942 by four professionals, Mr Champaklal Choksey, Mr Suryakant Dani, Mr Chimanlal Choksi and Mr Arvind Vakil. The company became India's largest paints manufacturer in 1968 and has held that position ever since.

In 1997, Champaklal Choksey and his son, Atul, sold their 8 per cent stake in the company because of differences with the other three promoter families who still own 53 per cent of the company. In India, Asian Paints controls around 42 per cent market share in the organised paints industry including around 55 per cent share in the decorative coatings and around 13 per cent share in the industrial coatings segment. The company operates in India through 106 depots and 27,000 dealers. The company also operates outside India through its subsidiaries Berger International Limited, Apco Coatings, SCIB Paints and Taubmans.

Asian Paint's superlative financial track record of strong

---

[11] Ambit Capital's research on Asian Paints.

revenue growth accompanied by rising profitability and strong cash generation have resulted in the firm leaving its rivals far behind. In each of the last six years, Asian Paints has gained market share, usually at the expense of its competitors.

CHART 2.1: Asian Paints' steady revenue growth and stable operating margins

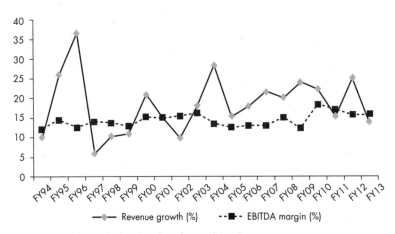

Source: Ambit Capital using data from Bloomberg.

CHART 2.2: Asian Paints' superior operating cash flows and healthy ROCEs

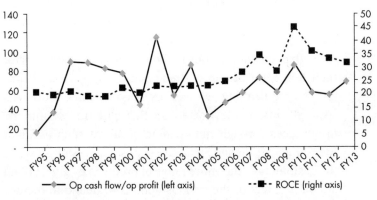

Source: Ambit Capital using data from Bloomberg.

Throughout the last ten years, Asian Paints' revenues have been three times as large as those of its nearest rival, Berger Paints, a well-run Kolkata headquartered company. Asian Paints' ability to maintain strong profit margins and strong return ratios over long periods of time (as evidenced by the charts above) and its ability to keep its strongest rival, Berger Paints, at bay point to strong competitive advantages. So what are these competitive advantages?

- **The leading brands in the sector**: Asian Paints' brand has become synonymous with paints in general in the minds of many Indian consumers. My colleague, Rakshit Ranjan's, discussions with dealers suggest that Asian Paints' brand recall in the decorative paints market is strong enough to compel dealers to stock Asian Paints' products in their stores irrespective of which brand the dealers wish to push to the customers. Also, Asian Paints is the only company in this sector which has strong recall for not only the parent brand (Asian Paints), but also for sub-brands like Royale, Apex, Apcolite, Utsav and Gattu. So how has the firm been able to create such strong brand recall?

  - Asian Paints carries out regular training programs for painters, especially for its more sophisticated emulsion products like Royale Play. A list of such trained painters is available to customers to ensure that high quality standards are maintained for application of the sophisticated paint products.

  - The Indian consumer's involvement in brand selection for a paint project has increased substantially over the past two decades. Most players have tried to capitalise on it through personalised consultation services to customers for their home, for example 'Home Solutions' by Asian Paints and 'Home Painting Services' by Berger Paints. Moreover, Asian Paints has leveraged on this shift in consumers' preferences through the opening of stores such as Color Ideas, Kids World and Signature stores. These stores expose the customers to the entire range of products by giving them a look and feel of the various options available to them if they wish to change the décor of their home.

- **Superior supply chain management**: Traditionally, the Asian Paints' strategy has been to diversify across geographies and products. Thus supply chain management has been a key area of focus for the management team. The firm has invested in the following initiatives in order to outperform its peers:
- **Use of technology for inventory management**: Asian Paints was among the early adopters of technology on the shop floor. In 1983 it started to automate the process of generating details of dispatches to the depots. Thereafter the firm invested in branch computerisation which, helped zonal distribution centers track their daily stock position levels. Also, between 1999 and 2002, the company invested in the implementation of supply chain management software from i2 technologies and enterprise resource planning solutions from SAP. This led to the integration of manufacturing plants, regional distribution centers and processing centers, thereby simplifying the tracking of demand and inventory levels across the country. These initiatives helped the company to improve the accuracy of demand forecasts (which helped lower inventory stock and working capital costs) and track the performance of dealers, take corrective action and incentivise the high performing dealers. Asian Paints' competitors have lagged Asian Paints in adopting such moves by 8–10 years.
- **High pricing power allows it to create a 'push-based' demand**: In anticipation of an upcoming product price hike from Asian Paints, dealers have historically been forced to stock up inventory levels in their shops a few weeks ahead of the seasonal spike in end consumer demand. For example, due to an expected 3–4 per cent price hike on 1 September 2012, dealers increased inventory levels at their stores by mid-August, thereby spreading out across time, the pressure of inventory management for Asian Paints in the high-demand period of September. Consequently, whilst 10 years ago Asian Paints would supply stocks to dealers in select tier 1 cities within a day (versus 4–5 days for peers), now the turnaround time has been reduced to 3–4 hours for Asian Paints (versus up to 1–2 days for its peers).

- **The best management team in the sector:** The intense focus on streamlining distribution and supply chain, and hence accelerated growth, has been driven by a combination of two key characteristics of the Asian Paints management team.
  - Asian Paints is the only paints company in the sector which has not seen a change in its controlling shareholder (promoter) over the past 70 years. All its competitors have seen: a) a change in the controlling shareholder; and b) significant presence of a foreign entity on the board of directors. This consistency at the Board level has helped Asian Paints maintain focus on the execution of a stable long term strategy.
  - The company has always focused on hiring and retaining high quality professionals. For example it was recruiting graduates from India's elite business schools even during 1970s. As a result, the middle management team at Asian Paints usually includes relatively young professionals who are in the age group of 40–45 years but have had 15–20 years of experience in the industry, mostly with Asian Paints.

Case study: TTK Prestige[12]

Incorporated in 1955, TTK Prestige, which is still majority owned by its promoter Mr TT Jagannathan, went public in 1994. It is now India's largest kitchenware company with sales of ₹13.6 billion in FY2013.

Until 1990, the company was selling only a single product, outer-lid aluminum pressure cookers with manufacturing facilities only in Bangalore and Hosur. The company then sought to build its export franchise through the 1990s only to come a cropper at the turn of the century when large customers, like Wal Mart, the giant US retailer, cancelled its order. By FY03, TTK Prestige was in serious financial trouble.

However, since then, the company has expanded its product offering and distribution channels to include a whole range

---

[12] Ambit Capital's research on TTK Prestige.

of cookers, cookware and kitchen appliances. Furthermore, additional manufacturing facilities have been created in Coimbatore, Roorkee and Vadodara and the company has made a sustained effort—through advertising and through building a salesforce and retail outlets—to expand its franchise outside its core southern Indian market.

The company currently sells all its products in India under the brand name 'Prestige' and exports pressure cookers, pressure pans and non-stick cookware to countries including the US, the UK and the Middle East under the brand name 'Manttra'.

CHART 2.3: TTK Prestige's revenue growth and operating margins

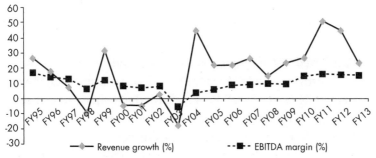

Source: Ambit Capital using data from Bloomberg.

CHART 2.4: TTK Prestige's operating cashflows and operating margins

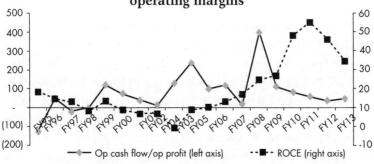

Source: Ambit Capital using data from Bloomberg.

As the charts above show, TTK Prestige's financial track record took a marked turn for the better post-FY2003 when the company decided to focus more intensely on the domestic market, expand its product range and build its own retail outlets. This strategy, combined with relatively healthy economic conditions, has resulted in strong revenue growth, expanding profit margins and expanding return ratios over the past decade. Furthermore, the firm has left its main rival, Hawkins, far behind. Ten years ago, TTK's revenues were 1.4 times that of Hawkins and now, that multiple is 3.2 times.

How has TTK Prestige fortified its business over the last ten years? What competitive advantages has it built?

- **Strong brand**: TTK Prestige enjoys strong brand recall across India with the brand being particularly popular in southern India. My colleague, Rakshit Ranjan's discussions with dealers reveal that in Bangalore TTK Prestige's brand is so strong that a traditional brown goods dealer tends to hang a banner of 'Prestige' outside the store in order to attract footfall even though he does not sell Prestige's products. In a product such as a pressure cooker where safety is of prime importance, healthy brand recall is a significant driver of sales.

- **Differentiated distribution channel–PSKs**: TTK Prestige's competitors sell their products either through the traditional brown goods dealer distribution model or through the supermarket channel. Whilst TTK Prestige also sells 80 per cent of its products through these two distribution channels, 20 per cent of the group's sales are currently made through the exclusive TTK Prestige franchisee Prestige Smart Kitchens (PSKs). The 500 PSKs, which have been developed over the last ten years, earn a 16 per cent retailing margin for selling TTK Prestige's products (this compares to the 20–25 per cent margin that the typical TTK Prestige dealer earns implying that TTK Prestige is at least 4 percentage points better off when its products are sold through PSKs).

- **Superior supply chain management**: Almost all brown goods dealers that my colleagues spoke to expressed disappointment with the supply chain management of TTK Prestige's main competitor compared to TTK Prestige. Most dealers said that the supply of TTK Prestige's products takes place within 2–4 days of the dealer raising demand for the stock, but delivery of the competitor's products can take anywhere between 2 weeks to 6 months. Consequently, several dealers in northern India say that proximity of the wholesale distributor and availability of the product at his store has been one of the biggest factors driving penetration of TTK Prestige's products in a market previously dominated by its competitor. TTK follows a hub-and-spoke supply chain model with 23 warehouses across India and a large number of wholesale distributors present across cities to cater to the demands for stock from all three distribution channels—retail supermarkets, traditional dealers and franchisee shops.

THE QUALITY OF THE FINANCIAL STATEMENTS

Financial analysis of the sort mentioned in the previous sub-section can only be done if the company's published financial performance is actually for real. If, on the other hand, the CEO is actively cooking the books in order to show investors what they want to see, the whole exercise of analysing the published accounts becomes futile. So how do professional investors determine whether a company's published accounts provide a 'true and fair' picture of its performance? A disproportionate amount of my time in India has been spent focusing on this vexed issue. My understanding is that most seasoned investors use a mix of the following basic 'tests' to establish their faith in the accounts:

- **Cash conversion ratio (Operating cash flows/Operating profit)**: Promoters around the world appreciate the importance of showing strong operating profits (i.e. earnings before interest costs, depreciation and amortization or EBITDA). Such profits are vital to propping up the share price which in turn helps the promoter raise fresh capital. One of the most effective ways of checking whether these profits are for real is to look at the ratio of EBITDA to operating cash flows (or CFO). Investors compare the CFO/EBITDA (also known as the 'cash conversion ratio') of the company with that of its peers. An even more effective test is to conduct this comparison using the last 4–5 years' financial statements. If the company in question has lower cash conversion than its peers over a 4–5 year period then the stated profits should be taken with a spoonful of salt.

- **The cash tax rate**: Another simple but effective check on the integrity of a listed entity's stated profits is the cash tax rate i.e. the amount of cash the business has paid to the exchequer as a percentage of profit before tax. Note that we are not talking here about the tax payment shown on the face of the P&L account; we are talking instead about the tax outgo in the company's cash flow statement (expressed as a percentage of PBT). If this rate is significantly lower than 30 per cent (the corporate tax rate in India is currently 34 per cent) for multiple years, it should raise a red flag about the reliability of the profits that the company is showing in its P&L. Genuine profits have to result, sooner or later, in a tax rate close to 34 per cent unless the firm in question has been given a tax exemption by the Government of India.

- **Loans and advances**: Most Indian promoters run multiple unlisted businesses (i.e. privately owned businesses alongside their listed business which are owned by a wide base of public shareholders). When these unlisted businesses need money, usually the handiest source of cash is the listed business. The easiest way to transfer cash from the listed to the promoter's unlisted business is via loans and advances. Hence, investors tend to keep an eye on the ratio of loans and advances to shareholders' equity. If, in an industry not known for requiring significant advances to customers or suppliers, the ratio loans and advances: shareholders' equity is consistently high then it could be suggestive of cash being pilfered from the listed business.

- **The identity of the auditor**: The last twenty years have shown that auditors the world over are susceptible to manipulation by promoters. Hence seasoned investors tend to focus on: (a) the identity of auditor—How reputable is the audit firm? Do they audit other large listed entities or are they auditing unlisted entities for the most part? Have they been involved in audit scandals before? Have they been pulled by the Registrar of Companies before? (b) the quantum of audit fees—how generous are the audit fees being paid by the firm in question compared to what its peers pay their auditors? (c) the quantum of non-audit fees paid to the audit firm—to what extent is the auditor receiving monies from the listed entity for other advisory services such as tax advice, payroll services or IT consultancy? If the non-audit fees overshadow the audit fees, that should raise a red flag.

My colleagues at Ambit Capital use a mixture of such ratios to establish the genuineness of the published financial statements of BSE 500 companies. Some of the world's largest investors make intensive use of our forensic accounting services as accounting quality seems to have a significant impact on shareholder returns. In particular, if we segment the BSE 500 into ten deciles based on accounting quality, the top decile of BSE 500 stocks on accounting quality outperforms the bottom decile by 26 per cent per annum.

THE PROMOTER'S COMPETENCE

'Nowadays, if I have significant questions about a management team, I will normally pass—there are lots of other companies that make the grade on this measure...It is very difficult to summarise what makes a good manager and how to assess this in a meeting, but the managements that normally impress me are those that have a detailed knowledge—strategically, operationally and financially. They tend to be fanatical about the business, working long hours and demanding high performance and excellence from their team and they are reasonably self assured and on top what they do without being arrogant... Generally, I like companies where managers have a decent

amount of 'skin in the game' in terms of shareholdings (I prefer shares to share options, which are much more of a one way bet).'—Anthony Bolton[13]

In a country such as India, where experienced, top flight managers are in short supply (particularly so for indigenous small-midcap companies), a company's main manager and supervisor is usually the promoter. Even if a promoter has installed what he calls a 'professional management team', four out of five times you can safely bet that the promoter is the guy who is really running the show. It follows, therefore, that his professional competence becomes central to his company's success. So how do the top professional investors do this?

The most common approach that I have seen seasoned investors take to assessing a promoter's competence is to meet the man (or, sometimes, the woman) at least 3–4 times over the span of a couple of years. In each of these meetings, investors are more or less trying to gauge the same three points:

• What did the promoter say six months or a year ago that he wanted to achieve over the next 1–2 years?
• How did the promoter say he would go about achieving these goals?
• Has he been actually able to achieve these goals in the manner that he wanted to? [14]

Given the extent of red tape and the deficient infrastructure that Indian businesses still have to deal with, executing clearly stated tasks within a pre-specified timeline is not easy—most promoters actually fail this test. Hence once an investor sees over a 1–2 year time frame that a specific promoter is broadly able to achieve what he set out to achieve, he usually ticks the 'promoter competence' box.

---

[13] *Investing Against the Tide*, Anthony Bolton, (FT Prentice Hall, 2009), pg 24.
[14] Thanks to BN Manjunath, whose interview is featured in this book, for helping me capture this framework succinctly.

The business that first set the benchmark for excellence in project execution was Reliance Industries Limited (RIL). Through the dark days of the 'license Raj' in the 1970s and 1980s, RIL was able to forge a path forward through the red tape that dragged India down in those decades. Whilst many have questioned the manner in which the firm managed to achieve its goals, its reputation for keeping its projects on track is legendary. The firm won over many sceptics when it managed to get back to business in just a couple of hours on 26 January 2001 after an earthquake measuring 7.9 on the Richter scale (the most severe earthquake to hit the subcontinent in the last 50 years) had shut down their Jamnagar refinery in Gujarat.

Jamnagar was then, and still is, the world's largest petrochemical refinery. Reliance's giant refinery had just been commissioned a year ago and in spite of the 2001 earthquake destroying property worth US$3 billion in the state of Gujarat, Reliance did not allow the refinery to be shut down for more than a few hours. The Reliance management worked flat out to ensure that power systems and other utilities were fully restored within a few hours of the earthquake. As a result a phased start-up of the plants in the refinery complex was activated the same day.

Over and above the efforts of the company's management on the day of the disaster, what allowed the Jamnagar refinery to get back to its feet so quickly is the amount Reliance had invested in disaster recovery systems. As a Mumbai-based newspaper put it, 'The refinery is equipped with electronic fences, CCTVs, data protection devices and smart card systems. The entire data is secured as a back-up at a centre in Hyderabad, to ensure continuity in case of a disaster. This focus on business continuity enabled the refinery to control the damage and resume its operations within just two days after a major fire erupted in one of its secondary units recently.'[15]

Other Indian businesses have sought to match RIL's execution excellence. Some examples are: Titan (the ability to produce and

---

[15] "How Reliance ensures the Jamnagar refinery stays on track", DNA, 6 July 2009.

retail world class luxury products), Kotak Mahindra Bank (the only Indian bank to credibly offer the full gamut of financial services products—from loans to insurance to investment banking), HDFC Bank (growth at a rapid clip while eschewing high levels of risk), Bajaj Auto (the first Indian manufacturer to build a large export franchise spanning Asia, Africa and Latin America). But Jamnagar remains the benchmark of world-class project execution in the Indian context.

THE PROMOTER'S INTEGRITY

'Even before you've ever met the management of a company, you normally have some perception about it. This is formed out of what you've read, heard or seen in different media. I give a lot of importance to what a newspaper says. There's no smoke without fire. Such a perception is more or less right. I start with that... When you go and personally meet the management, you notice the way they conduct themselves, what they share with you and what they don't, whether they come across as honest or deceptive. As you keep interacting with the management on a regular basis, say every three months, you are able to verify whether they deliver on their promises.' —Raamdeo Agrawal, Joint MD at Motilal Oswal Financial Services[16]

Around the world, several dynamic and industrious entrepreneurs have shown themselves to be modern day alchemists who can enter staid industries and build highly profitable enterprises (think of Karsanbhai Patel, the founder for washing powder giant, Nirma; think of Lakshmi Mittal of Ispat International; think of Sam Walton of Walmart). However, for every Patel, Mittal and Walton, there are dozens of charlatans who have taken their shareholders and staff for a ride using elaborate accounting shenanigans (think of the men behind Worldcom, Enron and Satyam).

---

[16] *India's Money Monarchs*, Chetan Parikh, (Capitalideasonline.com, 2005), pg 37.

In India this 'Dr Jekyll, My Hyde' split is even more commonly found as a weak legal system, overburdened regulators, intimidated auditors and ineffectual non-executive Board members seldom have the ability to stop a promoter intent upon enriching himself at the expense of other stakeholders. In fact, in sectors where government intervention is heavy—power, infrastructure, metals, mining, real estate, telecom, heavy engineering, airlines—a successful promoter, almost by definition and according to popular perception, has to be an individual who finds ways of circumventing the law in order to build a large, profitable enterprise. The challenge for minority shareholders is therefore especially acute in such sectors and the billion dollar question facing a long term minority investor is, *'Can I trust this promoter to look after my interests over the next 3–4 years?'*

Seasoned investors know that promoters can short change them in many ways, only one of which is through Satyam-style accounting shenanigans. A promoter, could for example, use his family owned companies to supply inputs to the listed entity at inflated prices or he could use family owned companies to buy finished products from the listed entity at depressed prices. He could, and this is a tried and tested manoeuvre in India, merge the listed entity with a family owned company at terms which favour the family owned company (thereby unduly diluting the minority investors in the listed business). More 'modern' promoters can issue ESOPs (or give performance-related pay awards) to themselves and other family members working in the firm using targets which are easy to meet. The list is endless—the fact is that the Indian promoter can whenever he wants to do so deprive minority investors of their rightful rewards.

So how do long term investors deal with this?

Firstly, successful investors tend to be hardened sceptics. They assume that everything that a promoter can theoretically do to shortchange minority shareholders, he will do. As Sanjoy Bhattacharya says, '...you have to make the assumption (which is unfortunate) that unless you have demonstrable proof on a long term basis that people are honest, they are crooks. This is cynical but it helps to save you from losses.'[17]

Secondly, investors look at the promoter's track record—has he done the sort of things mentioned in the preceding paragraph? If so, investors refuse to touch the shares of the tainted companies. Many of top investors in the Indian market will simply not buy the shares associated with some of the leading business families in the country because they can remember multiple episodes when the promoters of these businesses shortchanged minority investors. A business may be worth significantly more than its stock price but without an able and honest promoter, the value of the business is unlikely to be ever realised.

In case a promoter does not have a tainted past, the investor must closely check his or her credential and ask whether a need will arise for the promoter to shortchange investors. In the run up to a QIP (Qualified Institutional Placement) or a merger which will be paid for in shares, most investors know that most promoters will do whatever they can to inflate the share price. So the risk really arises on the other side of the corporate event. In such circumstances, investors tend to look for how meaningful the promoter's commercial interests are outside the listed entity. The larger these interests, the more fragile their profitability, the greater the tendency for investors to avoid such promoters.

Finally, many successful investors have taken the view that they will avoid all listed companies in India where the promoters are close to the political apparatus. Proximity to politicians not only creates the need to transfer money from the listed entity to gratify the powers that be, it also breeds in the promoter's mind the sense that he is above and beyond the law.

---

[17] *India's Money Monarchs*, Chetan Parikh, (Capitalideasonline.com, 2005), pg 72.

'WE WILL NOT BUY A STOCK THAT IS TOO EXPENSIVE'

Alroy Lobo *is Chief Strategist and Global Head of Equities at Kotak Mahindra Asset Management Company. Other than the four years that he was at Godrej & Boyce during his initial years, Alroy has spent almost his entire career in Uday Kotak's financial services empire. He has been instrumental in making Kotak Mutual Fund one of the top 10 mutual fund houses in India.*

How did you enter the stockmarket?

AL: It was quite by accident because none of the members in my family were in the stock market or even close to investing. Even when I did my management studies in Finance, I never had the stock market in mind. After completing my studies, in 1988 I actually joined a manufacturing concern, Godrej & Boyce.

I worked for them until 1992 in Vikhroli (a suburb of Mumbai). Initially I was in the Management Services division doing projects for various departments but very quickly I moved into the Purchase department and my job was vendor development. Godrej had a number of plants—18–20 if I am not mistaken—and they wanted us to create a vendor development cell almost from scratch. Our job was to assess the various vendors. We started with a team with 2 members and then we added a member; so the 3 of us were the vendor development cell. What we used to do was visit Godrej & Boyce's suppliers and do a complete assessment. For this we created a complete vendor assessment model.

So this was part of 'quality control'?

AL: No, not so much. Our first job was to find out whether the vendor has premises to manufacture his output or was he getting the work done from somewhere else. Secondly, if he is the manufacturer then what kind of machine set up does he have. Is he the right guy to do business with? Does he have financial capability? Does he have workers of respectable quality? Does he have the required tools, quality control...everything? We created a complete framework for a vendor evaluation model, assessed them on a point scale. I visited nearly 3,000 companies in those 4 years. I saw the small scale industry at very close quarters and I wrote reports on 1,600 companies. We created vendor rating systems, even created estimation techniques—how do you do costing of a product based on the assessment, the machine rates and other things. It was quite a good experience for me. During the course of that, during lunch hours, there were a few guys who were interested in stock markets and they started talking about investments. That's the time I started hearing about stock markets and I started thinking about investing personally.

So you first started investing when you were at Godrej & Boyce?

AL: Yes. There was a friend of mine who would evaluate the Union Budget. Once when I was watching the Budget with him, I found it quite interesting to see the impact it had on markets. I invested but it was not much. We did not earn much at the time. My first investment was in a company called Ponni Sugars. I didn't lose money but I learnt a lot. I made a lot of mistakes personally at the time but some of them were good winners. Overall I got very interested in the field and thought *'why can't I make this a profession?'*

Then I began searching for employment in this field and I joined a very small company which you would not hear of today. It was called HMG Financial Services. They were into investment banking and broking. I was their first research analyst...this was 1992 December. It was a small set-up up and after about 9 months I decided to move out. That was when I got a job at Kotak Securities which was called 'Uday S Kotak' at the time. It had not been corporatised into Kotak Securities yet.

I joined them in 1993 September. Although they had a broking license, they had both retail and institutional broking together—they had not split the two types of broking up at that time. I remember the first day I came in and I was made to write reports on companies that I had not studied before and the report was based all on secondary information—from newspapers and magazines. We used to assess the information available in the press and do a four line P&L statement: Net sales, Operating Profit, PBT, PAT and EPS.

Was that because you did not have access to annual reports in those days?

AL: Well we did have annual reports but access to these reports was tricky because there was no Internet access at the time. We had to work with whatever we could get—we did not have the full library of annual reports. Over time we began coming out with one-pagers on companies. As yet, these were not detailed reports but we had a nice product at the time called *India Profile* which would contain an industry study and reports on 2–3 companies in the industry. I remember writing my first *India Profile* on the dye industry and I did a report on Color Chem. The next was on the sugar industry and so on. Gradually our reports became detailed but they were still P&L focused, not cash flow focused and did not have too much balance sheet analysis.

After one or two years of working like this, we realised that balance sheet matters, cash flow matters and somewhere around 1994–1995 Goldman Sachs announced a tie-up with Kotak. Goldman had a very strong understanding of how global investors look at research and we started getting that perspective from Goldman. Remember, at that stage, we at Kotak had no sector analysts; anyone who grabbed a company did a report. Once Goldman came in we had to have a sector focus and I happened to get the pharma industry because no one else was willing to take it. I had covered some pharma companies in the past and so the management of our brokerage said that *'since you have done this why don't you take up this sector?'* I covered that for a long time. Actually, Goldman taught us a lot about how to write a research report, what the international investor is looking for and what we need to focus on.

Was it classroom training that the people from Goldman imparted?

AL: No, there was a gentleman from Goldman who used to come down to our Mumbai offices quite regularly. He was a mentor and the head of research. He used to vet our reports and he gave us a hard time when each of us gave him our first report. But once you got your first report through, life became easier as you understood what he was looking for and what he was trying to teach us. I remember my first report was Dr Reddy's and it took a long time for me to get it passed. It took three months but after that it was a cakewalk because then I understood what was needed. I think we got into the rhythm of what global investors wanted quite early in the game.

I presume Kotak's JV with Goldman Sachs was the first JV between an Indian broker and a major foreign broker?

AL: Yes, we were the first big global JV at the time. To give you a sense of how early we were in the game, at that time the only big foreign institutional investor in India was Jardine Fleming and then you had Morgan Stanley coming in. That's when we started doing very serious research in India. As we ourselves got aligned sectorally, we hired more people.

This would be in 1994–1995?

AL: Yes, because when I joined Kotak, there was hardly anyone in research. I would have been the second guy hired. Also, between my hiring and the Goldman JV, we had separated retail and institutional broking and I became a part of the latter.

How were you valuing stocks at that time?

AL: We were more focused on PE and I would say that we were more relative valuation focused than absolute valuation focused. But as we became sectorally focused, we began to do a lot of work to project the cash flows, balance sheet and the P&L statements completely. All three were estimated in great detail and Goldman had a nice thing where everything you wrote in your report had to have a justification. So if you wrote sales would grow at 15 per cent you had to say why...if you said operating profit was going up you had to have a note why you were saying that. Every part of the P&L and cash flow statement had to be justified. That taught us a lot.

Reports used to be quite thick at the time. I think the biggest report I had written in the Goldman years was on Wipro which was 75 pages. Even as I was covering pharma, I began getting interested in software as an industry. At the time it was very small and there was lot of resistance from our management to take up the sector. It was like *'why don't you take steel or cement, they are the big sectors, where turnover is high and broking commissions are high?'*

I was sure that the software sector had the potential to grow very big. Even in pharma, the sector was not too big and there was no investment banking business in that sector. So from a commercial perspective both these sectors were not great but I felt they were promising sectors from an Indian perspective. There was also debate (because I had picked up suitable experience in pharma) about whether I should do software or cement. I did not want to give up software. So I decided to do both—cement and software. Later on these sectors became so big that I handed over cement and just did pharma and software.

You began covering the software sector in 1995–1997?

AL: I would say in 1995 I wrote my first significant report on software but the really big reports started coming in 1997 by which time we had built very detailed financial models on these companies. By then we literally designed an entire model on how to evaluate a software company, how to build a model for a software company through understanding of how each company works, etc. My first software report was on Satyam. At that time Satyam was a very small company. It had a profit of about ₹1.5 crore out of which close to ₹1 crore came from 'other income'. But we forecast that this would be a ₹100 crore turnover company within a certain time frame. Satyam hit that milestone earlier than I had predicted.

By the mid-1990s, the software industry was growing very fast. A lot of software companies went public and we got involved in writing research reports for investment banking deals and IPOs. I gave up cement and focused on pharma and software which became really big sectors for Kotak's broking franchise. Once we started doing more detailed analysis of sector, we started conducting free cash flow analysis and started reducing our dependence on relative valuation and building absolute valuation models. I think we were ahead of the market in terms of our understanding of the software sector. We had access to very senior people within companies who at this point in time may not be very easily accessible—but they were at that time because they were part of smaller companies. Nobody expected the software industry to be so big. As we approached the turn of the century, the dotcom wave obviously became very big. Valuations reached astronomical levels. I remember Wipro was trading at 300 PE, Infosys at 200 PE, Hughes Software Systems at 100 PE and there were investment banking pitches that were going anywhere between 40–70 PE. That was the state of the industry.

In the midst of this frenzy, there was only one investor who I remember was asking whether the software industry could grow at this pace for such a long period of time as reflected in analysts' estimates. I think everyone else forgot that no company in the world has delivered such earnings growth over such a long period of time. At the time demand was taken to be given and we were only worried about supply. Things changed so rapidly after that as there was no demand and only supply! The other by-product of the dotcom boom was that we expanded our software team. From one man covering software we became a three man team. I had got involved in a lot of marketing and pitching for investment banking deals. So we had to hire other people. After some time software became so big that I had to give up covering the pharma sector. We enjoyed that phase as the focus was on educating institutional investors about the Indian software sector. I remember my first report for FIIs was explaining what is on-site and offshore and why offshore gives you better margins. Very basic stuff, right? My first report on pharma was to explain how the Indian industry works. What is process patent, product patent? What is bulk drug and what is formulation? Once we had explained the basic stuff, we took our research to a very advanced stage. So we did a lot of education sessions with a lot of investors.

Gradually, both the investment industry and the broking industry started evolving, growing and different players came in. As competition grew, we did very differentiated reports. My first report on Infosys was not the first on the company in the industry. But whilst everybody covered Infosys, nobody did it well. So we said can we split up the onsite and offshore profitability for Infosys and show investors how these two P&Ls and balance sheets really work. That report went down well with investors.

There was a time in pharma when a lot of MNCs were trading at 40 PEs and Indian pharma companies were trading at 10–15 PEs. We did a report that said that the entire valuation framework needs to be reassessed because Indian companies had greater potential as their export avenues were an open-ended growth channel which the MNCs in India did not have. We also pointed out that the Indian pharma companies were doing a lot of basic research, a lot of R&D and we said that their valuations should converge with MNCs. We kept doing such reports that were leading the industry thought process.

By the turn of the century, the majority of your clients were FIIs?

AL: A large amount was. Domestic investors were not very big in those days plus FIIs were very keen to invest in India. I remember in software there was one client who wanted to buy all the software companies in India—from the bottom player to the top ones. During those years even a company like Wipro was not very liquid—only 200 shares traded per day. So even if he liked the company, he could not buy it. I remember we had an order for one lakh shares of Wipro but we could not fill it because only 200 shares were traded that day. Infosys was the darling in those days, TCS was not even listed.

I was fortunate to be associated with most of the software companies when they got listed—Polaris, iFlex, Ramco Systems,

Mascot Systems, TCS, Tech Mahindra, etc. This gave us access to the management teams and their business models. To a large extent we played the role of guiding the thought process in the software industry. We focused on seeing trends ahead of the market and on positioning companies accordingly—we did not just speak to the top management, we spoke to the divisional business heads of each of these companies. As an analyst for every company tracked, I would say I spoke to at least 8–10 people in these companies on a regular basis (over and above speaking to the top management). Over time we identified a lot of fraud cases too. In those days, even dodgy companies wanted the 'software' tag for the valuations that would come with it.

How did you deal with the challenge that most analysts struggle to come to terms with, namely, how am I going to write great research and spend enough time with investors?

AL: It was a straightforward thing. During those days a lot of investors used to call us rather than we calling them—we were ahead of the industry and the investors knew we did path-breaking work. Since we were also involved in a lot of IPOs, I had gone marketing around the world repeatedly and a lot of people got to know me. Whenever they wanted to know anything they would call me. We used to call a few clients but there were not too many. It was not as if we had wide investor base. Also we had very large clients and that made us a rarity: a local house with access to very large global clients. Goldman as partner also gave us leverage but a lot of hard work went in from the Kotak team.

How did you maintain the independence of your research and of your thought process?

AL: By the turn of the century, we had built a very good research team. I would say that we have always built in bad times. The best analysts—even from MNCs—joined us because we did independent research. Even though we had a large investment banking arm, they never influenced our research. At times investment banking business may have been lost but the company culture was 'do what is right for your client'. A lot of people who knew that came and joined us and they were very happy because the work content at Kotak was very rich. It was not about compensation as much as work content. Everybody in the team was an authority on the subject that he/she covered and we had a clear view that we were the best research team. We added a lot of value for our clients: we did a lot of original work and almost all of it was based on primary data digging. We then did a lot of roadshows to sell this work.

We got a lot of satisfaction and we slogged it out. The days were long—the morning meeting was at 8 am, we left home at 7 am and were reaching home at 9–10 pm. During results season we were reaching home at 3 am! Road shows were hectic too. Later on, I also started doing strategy and then I gave some of the sectors to others, but I remember doing at least 6 road shows in a year to the Far East, 4 to the US and Europe. So even ten years into my brokerage career, I was doing 10 roadshows a year.

How did you manage the research workload while you were travelling?

AL: Whilst we did lots of marketing, we had lots of time to write also. We empowered our juniors to do high quality work to groom them as good analysts. As we became senior it became difficult for us to do a lot of things but we created what are called 'control sheets' in our financial models. Looking at a control sheet would give me a good sense of the quality of the back-end of the model. Furthermore, there was no report in Kotak that was not vetted by the head of research. I was head at the time. I moved from analyst to head of research.

This was in 2000–01?

AL: I was co-head of research in late nineties and 2000–01 would have been head of research. But every report was run past me and this was not just for software or pharma. Even for banking, industrials, autos—every report would be vetted by me. This quality check was great because we made a lot of the mistakes but those mistakes were never in the final versions of the report.

Every analyst knew the Kotak way and I remember in those days we even went to cell level evaluation of the Excel models of our analysts. We would take the model, see cell wise how he was doing things. We didn't want hard coded stuff inside; we wanted things to be parameterised. We wanted assumptions to be modular. So we created a standardised structure for the tabs in a company-specific financial model because we were running a very interesting model which I will come to in a moment. I think everybody in the team followed the Kotak way; they knew this was the way to do it.

Somehow or the other, even after the turn of the century, there was still a lot of focus on P&L and EPS and investing. How do we change the mindset to a cash flow/balance sheet mindset? That's a question that bothered my colleagues and myself. That's the time we started working on something very very interesting.

We clearly saw that if a company had a good cash flow profile—a growing cashflow profile to be specific—that had a big impact on stock prices. We did a rudimentary exercise where we looked at the mistakes we made where we recommended companies that had good EPS growth but never performed in stock markets. We found that cash flow was very important relative to EPS for stock market performance.

Then in 2001 we performed a much bigger crunch and established comprehensively that cash flow is important. That is the time when we said 'let us see if we can scale this up into a full-fledged model and computerise it'. That's when we created 'Whizdom'. It is a free cash flow momentum tool linked to the company-specific models created by the analysts. If you run a discounted cashflow (DCF) model to value a company, the problem is that the value could be back-ended or front-ended. Whizdom clearly tells you where the value is. And it very clearly defines what is a value stock, what is a re-rating stock, what is profit booking stock, growth stock—everything was very well defined with numbers and computerised and then we had another overlay which was reverse DCF to see whether if a company's reported free cash flow momentum is already in the price. Whizdom is very powerful and is being used even today by Kotak Institutional

Equities. The model initially ran with our estimates and later we put it on our dashboards for clients to parameterise their numbers and assumptions and see what the model tells them.

We used Whizdom to make the entire mindset change within the Institutional Equities group to look at free cash flow management. So if I am looking at Whizdom I can look at all the analyst's estimates on free cash flow basis within the system and tell the analyst whether something looks odd. Slowly we started getting our free cash flow estimates right. For us getting the free cash flow estimates right was more important than getting EPS right. That changed the entire perspective on how we looked at companies and it was scalable—at the time we were looking at 130–150 companies and all the analysts' models were linked to Whizdom.

Let me get this clear—to this day the market does not focus on free cash flow. So if the Kotak analyst forecasts cash flow correctly, does that really help him given that that is not the market's focus?

AL: See, it helps get your calls right. From the market perspective, they want your calls right, they want your target prices to be right. So I remember in those days we used to say that this is what our analysts are recommending and this is what Whizdom is saying. Many times there was a disconnect between the two and we used to put it out openly. The reason for this is that there may be times when analysts are looking at short term triggers. Whizdom sees two years ahead at least and sees the change before the analyst can see it. There was a company called VSNL (now a Tata company) and it had a lot of cash in its balance sheet and everyone said it was a great value stock. Whizdom model showed that in the next two years there would be an erosion of the entire cash and hence there would be heavy value destruction over the next two years. So we said that in the next two years value is going to be destroyed and assuming there is no growth based on existing cash flows, this is the value of the company. That helped our clients understand that the company would be de-rated.

Whizdom is still running. It is a fantastic piece of work and it changed our organisation's mindset. If you come to asset management side of the business, then you see that the focus is still on growth and PE multiples based investing. Cash flows are looked at but not as we did in Whizdom where cash flows are the heart of the valuation process. So much so that at that time many investors said that 'in every report, can you give us the Whizdom view also instead of just the EPS perspective'. It was a very good franchise builder for us.

In the years 2003–2005, Kotak Institutional Equities invested heavily in systems and process. We created another software asset from scratch, a product called AKSESS, with a budget of ₹5 lakh. All our research was archived. All our morning flashes were done through that product automatically including editing, compliance clearance, etc. We also profiled clients in the system and only sent those reports that were needed by that specific client. We used tech solutions heavily to help clients.

I remember our first big conference. For the coordination of meetings, slots, one-on-ones between investors and companies— the entire thing was done by the analysts at zero cost. Everything was done in house. We had some good guys, who went beyond the analysts' duties. Visual Basic was learned and software was developed in house. We were a big family in Kotak. There was no one on the street we thought was better than us. Over time we got recognition within the firm and from our clients.

I took up strategy in 2001 and I remember that my first report on strategy was a 300 pager. Out of those 300 pages maybe about 30–40 pages was actual strategy and the rest was about sector, companies, etc. was a big thick book which some found difficult to read. It was my first strategy report and I wanted to make that impact. Then slowly I gave up the software sector. But somehow down the line I think based on organisational need, I came back to the tech sector. So at some point I was working on both strategy and tech.

I started working on tech with another analyst—Kawaljeet— now head of research Kotak Institutional Equities. Then once everything was in shape, I went back into the strategy in 2001. In 2007, I joined the asset management firm.

How did you find the move to asset management?

AL: In the asset management side there was a disconnect between the time frames people were using. In India mutual funds are sold not bought. You need distributors to market your fund. So if you are not a good performing fund you go off the radar. Unless you have a long track record (and hence the investors are willing to give you time to make mistakes), you have to produce results consistently over shorter time frames. The time frames that you have been used to 12 months, 2–3 years—start getting crunched even though we believe the investment must be done from a long term perspective. That mindset still exists in the mutual fund industry. As a result you don't have too many funds who can take the really long term calls. This has created an opening for private equity set ups which are entering listed market equity investing. I think that is the best way to make money for our investors.

In the mutual fund industry, there is a tendency to try and catch every big move in the market in the short term which is difficult as stock performances over the investment horizon may not be linear but lumpy. Having said that, the same thinking around free cash flow based valuation that I mentioned in the context of our Institutional Equities has been brought by us to the asset management business. That's been our philosophy. We are focused on valuation, businesses and managements. We are not value investors in that we don't buy stocks just because they are very cheap. They have to be good businesses with good managements and available at good valuations. All three boxes have to be ticked.

How well did this approach work in the 7–8 months following the post-Lehman recovery (March-November 2009) when no one cared about cash flow?

AL: I won't say that the philosophy had completely evolved fully in the asset management business at the point. However, that period brings out another important facet of investing. At any point in time, an investor needs to understand what the market is focusing on. If you are focused on a specific idea or theme and the market is not willing to buy that theme, you will get the stock call completely wrong. The important thing is to know what the market is thinking.

At the same time, we are playing in uncharted waters and don't know when things could change. We should be alert about when to change. At the end of all this what you realise is—and normally this is when markets are going nowhere for five or six years—that if you stick to your investment philosophy and even if these aberrations happen in between, you can still make money on a long term basis. It is just that the set up in a mutual fund industry does not give you that chance. That forces you to change the philosophy and go with the flow and that's when the problem begins. The way mutual funds are evaluated is that investors and distributors look at the track record but that does not tell you what your future performance is going to be. If someone is number one and has taken excessive risk to be number one then next year he could be ranked last. That means there has to be far greater assessment of the portfolios, far deeper understanding of investment philosophies but that does not happen. As a result ultimately the funds that get money are those that do well for one year or three year period with the belief that they will do well in next one to three years also. But there are funds that have done well for ten years also and to do that they have followed a philosophy. Now we are coming to the clear understanding that we need to stick to our philosophy. We don't deviate, unless there is a big disruption that happens and creates a major opportunity for us.

What is your selling philosophy?

AL: We have our price targets for each holding and we will respect those price targets.

So even with a star stock, like Eicher Motors, the selling discipline will be maintained if the price target is hit?

AL: We will take profits on the stock and bring down the overweight in the portfolio if our price target is met. If the stock goes up after that, we will go underweight. There have been many good companies where we have exited after a sharp rally in the price and then re-entered later when the share price has corrected.

There is a school of thought that with certain high quality stocks, like HDFC Bank, one should not sell even if the stock is overvalued. Do you subscribe to that?

AL: No. We have changed weights in HDFC Bank also. It is a good bank but if it is too expensive then we will cut and similarly with Sun Pharmaceuticals which is a fantastic company but there are times when you get it cheap. Once there was an announcement that the company had to pay a penalty. That brought Sun's share price down and we bought more. Those are the opportunities we look for. But we will not chase a stock that is too high priced. For growth stocks we are willing to look a little more ahead. For good companies rather than only one year, we look at two years. But we will not discount five years...we are very disciplined...but we generally like companies that have a good returns profile...We don't mind buying companies with a low return if we believe the ROEs and ROCEs are going to be trending upwards. Similarly, we are willing to buy free cash flow negative companies if we can see the free cash flow turning positive. That's how the Whizdom model actually works.

With some of our core holdings, we will keep changing the overweights. For example, we have increased and decreased TCS' weight over time but it has always been in the portfolio. At this point in time in Kotak Asset Management, we have been through an evolution, learnt, got a good framework, got more confident about consistency and predictability.

When you look at the portfolios of the top 10 mutual funds in India what do you see?

AL: The funds that do extremely well are concentrated rather than diversified. You normally find such funds in the midcap segment.

They don't adhere to a benchmark. The second is that there is a fair amount of illiquidity that is built into these portfolios. This is a risk in tough times but when the going is good the rewards are good because you get an illiquidity premium in your returns.

What we have done is created a risk framework so that we don't get into bad quality, illiquid names and don't build up very high concentration risk. For those investors who want that kind of thing, we have specialists who can do that but our frontline funds have strict quality, liquidity and concentration criteria.

Our strength lies in our research and in the experience of our fund managers to use our research effectively. We also use good analysts on the sell-side effectively to make informed decisions. We are run almost like a sell-side firm even on the buy-side. For all our stocks, we have cash flow based models and cash flow based valuations. When I am looking at a stock, the first thing I look at is the Kotak Asset Management analyst's numbers.

Would you say that the distinction between buy-side (i.e. fund management) and sell-side (i.e. broking) is more superficial than real?

AL: Different buy-side firms have different approaches. There is one school that says that you don't need a research team on the buy-side at all. Just talk to a good sell-side analyst and get their models and that is all. Another school of thought on the buy-side is that a few people should interact with the sell-side and relay the messages to the senior member of the investment team. We call this 'postman research'. We have taken a very different route.

We build our models from scratch. There is complete control from our end. If you ask our buy-side analyst where a specific number is coming from, he will give you an answer in great detail and that is a big differentiator. Our analysts are experienced and do a good job. It took us a long time to build this mindset for investment, to be singularly focused, to give analysts time to build models. Until then we looked at sell-side research. But now we have a potent combination of sell and buy-side analysts. We have a good evaluation model for the sell-side: we use third party models in addition to our own to evaluate the sell-side. The sell-side analyst is more in-depth because they do a few companies in detail. The buy-side analyst has to cover far more stocks. We have tried to bring the same kind of rigour to our buy-side but it is tough because there are many more names: our buy-side analyst covers 30 stocks compared to the 15 that a typical sell-side analyst has to cover.

THREE

Simple Rules for Successful Investing

'Rules are for the obedience of fools and the guidance of wise men.'—David Oglivy, 'The Father of Advertising'[1]

'We really can say "no" in 10 seconds or so to 90 per cent of all the things that come along simply because we have these filters.'—Warren Buffett[2]

Whenever I have the privilege of interviewing a freshly minted chartered accountant or a brand new business school graduate, I ask him why he wants to work in the stock market. After all, there are many other professions which are worth pursuing. A doctor, for example, not only saves lives but also builds a financially secure future for himself. A management consultant can not only enrich himself but, if he rises up the ranks, can end up becoming the advisor to and confidant of the captains of industry. A professional sportsperson or entertainer can not only earn fame and fortune but also travel around the world and mingle with people from other cultures and countries. So why enter the stock market when there are so many other meaningful vocations to pursue?

---

[1] *Investing Against the Tide,* Anthony Bolton, (FT Prentice Hall, 2009), pg 11.
[2] *Investing Against the Tide,* Anthony Bolton, (FT Prentice Hall, 2009), pg 11.

The answers I got were a critical driver of my writing this book. There is an image out there, not just amongst young people, but also with the public at large that the stock market is a casino where gamblers and operators roll the dice and where, those with inside information have an edge. This is unfortunate because not only does this deter millions of individuals from investing their savings in stocks (and fuels India's unhealthy obsession with gold and real estate), it also draws young professionals to the stock market for all the wrong reasons (primary amongst them being a desire to 'get rich quick').

The reality of long term success in the stock market is very different. Whilst there are some investors who rely upon inside information to make money, truly successful long term investors use other techniques to make money. In fact, one sure way to lose money in the market (and get into trouble with the law) is to rely upon inside information. Successful long term investors use a simple but powerful set of rules to make money in the market. We will look at these rules in detail in this section and then, in the next section, delve into the mental discipline required to adhere to them.

RULES FOR BUYING

Rule 1: Only buy a stock if you understand the business model.

> 'I also prefer very simple businesses. If the business model is very difficult to understand, I'm happy to pass on it—there are lots of others that are easy to understand.'—Anthony Bolton.[3]

Before you can start assessing the merits of a business, you need to understand the product that the company manufactures. You need to answer simple questions such as 'who buys it, why does he buy it and how does the company make money'. Therefore,

---

[3] *Investing Against the Tide,* Anthony Bolton, (FT Prentice Hall, 2009), pg 11.

the most basic buying rule is to not even consider a company for investing, if you do not 'understand' the business.

This process of understanding how a company works is not as simple as it sounds. Let me illustrate with a couple of examples. Let's take what sounds like a simple business such as pressure cookers and focus on the market leader, TTK Prestige. Most people believe that TTK Prestige manufactures only one product, pressure cookers, and manufactures this largely in India and sells it through third party distributors in India. Hence it is, you would imagine, a fairly simple business to understand and invest in. However, because of the metamorphosis that TTK has been through in the past decade or so, the reality is very different (not just for TTK Prestige but for a host of other Indian consumer durables manufacturers):

- Only a third of TTK's revenues now arise from pressure cookers; the remaining two-thirds of revenues come from selling a variety of kitchenware products such as non-stick cookware (17 per cent of total revenues), kitchen electrical appliances (33 per cent of total revenues) and gas stoves (9 per cent of total revenues).
- Around a quarter of TTK's revenues come from products manufactured in China by outsourced suppliers. At its peak in FY12, as much as 40 per cent of its revenues arose from products sourced by TTK from Chinese manufacturers.
- As much as a fifth of TTK's revenues are generated from sales through Prestige Smart Kitchens (PSK). These are stores owned and operated by franchisees which showcase the entire Prestige product range from pressure cookers to induction cook-tops and electrical appliances. TTK Prestige frequently uses the PSK network to either launch new products or expand its presence in smaller cities where the traditional multi-brand dealer distribution network is not strong enough. The credit terms or capex support available to PSKs consequently depend on the perceived demand pull for TTK products in the region.
- Six per cent of TTK's revenues (and an even higher percentage

of its profits) arise from exports (as of FY13). This figure is up from 2 per cent a couple of years ago.

These four facets of TTK's business—multiple products (rather than just pressure cookers), sourced from multiple countries, sold through multiple channels (including their own 'Smart Kitchen' stores and sold in multiple countries—has helped accelerate the firm's growth in revenue terms over the past decade (FY03–13 revenue CAGR of 28 per cent), increase its EBITDA margins (minus 5 per cent in FY03 to 15 per cent in FY13), sweat its fixed assets (i.e. its plant and machinery harder) and shorten its working capital cycle. The overall result is not just a surge in profitability (FY04–13 EPS CAGR of 105 per cent) but also acceleration in operating cash flow (FY03–12 operating cash flow CAGR of 64 per cent).

The three critical 'value levers' for TTK therefore have become:

1. **Product innovation**: Over 70 per cent of TTK Prestige's revenues in any given year are generated from items introduced over the previous three years. This helps the company in two ways: (a) Introduce differentiated products which are better aligned with evolving customer preferences compared to the products offered by competitors; and(b) Leverage the strength of its existing brand and distribution to enter into new categories of kitchenware and hence widen the effective size of the market that TTK Prestige caters to.

2. **Distribution and supply chain management**: With 23 warehouses across India and an efficient hub and spoke distribution network in place, dealers across India acknowledge that in stark contrast to most of its competitors, availability of stock on demand is seldom a concern with TTK Prestige's products. Moreover, franchisee shops (PSKs), help distribute the entire product range, increase competition with traditional dealers, and help TTK penetrate into cities where brand awareness remains low.

3. **Talented and well incentivised management team**: TTK Prestige's senior management, led by the promoter, TT Jagannathan, is strongly focused on maintaining the company's pre-tax ROCE of 50 per cent. He ensures that the management

team is aligned to the same goals and that the company offers sufficient incentives to the team for their efforts. The team consists of high quality home-grown professionals who took control of various senior level responsibilities a decade ago once the firm realised that it was too big to be run single-handedly by TT Jagannathan. Moreover, the company is now in the process of creating several middle management roles to handle the scale of business it targets to achieve in the coming years. Given the transition from a solely promoter-managed company to one which is managed by professionals, the firm has put in place performance based incentive structures for the professionals in order to allow them to increase their shareholding in the firm in the coming years.

Let's take another example, Infosys, the large IT services company. Surely, I hear you say, given the amount that has been written on this sector, by now the IT services business is easy to understand—the vendor finds corporate customers in the West and then uses talented but low-cost programmers in India to write applications for these corporations. The vendor then installs this application in the offices of the Western company and gets paid a recurring amount as development and maintenance fees for its services on an hourly basis and, on rare occasions, an upfront license fee.

The reality of the Infosys business is very different.

- Only a third of the company's revenues are from the sort of Application Development and Maintenance (ADM) mentioned in the previous para. The other third of its revenues arise from Consulting and System Integration, while functions such as Testing (9 per cent of revenues), Remote Infrastructure Management (7 per cent), BPO (6 per cent) and Products (5 per cent) account for the rest.

- Only 70 per cent of Infosys' employees are in India; the rest are spread around the world with major development centres in US, Latin America, Australia, China, UK and western European countries. Furthermore, with increasing focus on local employment by Western economies, IT services companies need to increase the proportion of local staff in their customer locations overseas.

- A significant percentage of its revenues (43 per cent) are now from fixed price contracts where revenues have a weaker correlation with employee headcount (compared to 'time and material' contracts where there is a direct correlation between revenues and headcount). Indeed, there has been rising demand for 'outcome based pricing', where the vendor is rewarded based on savings generated for the clients. Furthermore, around 5 per cent of Infosys' revenues come from Non-Linear Products, Platform and Solutions businesses. All these developments indicate that Indian IT outsourcing is no longer just a body shopping business.

- Historically, agreements in the IT business allowed vendors to pass on the compensation paid to their staff for cost of living adjustments (COLA) to the customer. However, as the IT services industry matured, the balance of power shifted towards the customers. As a result, nowadays customers simply do not want to countenance COLA-related price hikes. This impacts the IT vendor's margins (since the vendor can no longer pass on the higher cost of wages to the customer) and the only way to deal with such margin pressure is for firms like Infosys to become far more focused on costs.

- Emerging technologies that have powered a slew of interactive tools and products (Social Networks, Media, 'Big Data' Analytics and Cloud Computing) are disrupting the traditional IT services business model. The conventional license model is transitioning into a 'pay-as-you-use' model that implies smaller contract sizes for IT services firms.

In light of these changes to the IT services business, the three critical 'value levers' for Infosys therefore have become:

Solutions led approach: Given that the old business of providing Application Development and Maintenance (ADM) business through skilled resources at low cost has become commonplace, providing 'solutions' (as opposed to providing programming talent) becomes the key to remaining competitive.

Focus more on cost efficiencies: As mentioned above, Infosys' customers have become far more price sensitive than they were, say, five years ago. As a result, the firm has to stay focused on managing costs by sharing resources (across projects and across verticals), by using 'just-in-time' hiring, by consolidating offices and by using automation (i.e. replacing programmers with software which can be used to write software).

Building for Social, Mobile, Analytics and Cloud based services (SMAC): The precise size of the SMAC opportunity might be hard to gauge, given the pervasive influence of these innovations on our lives. But it is clear that more and more IT services solutions will have to focus on emerging technologies. Infosys too needs to invest in developing these capabilities—either organically or inorganically to create future drivers of growth.

These two case studies—TTK Prestige and Infosys—help illustrate that the ability of a firm to add value, in the context of the world around it, is at the core of its ability to generate high ROCEs (and hence central to its ability to reward its shareholders). Over the past decade, in a relatively stable industry—kitchenware—TTK Prestige has innovated systematically and, by and large, successfully, to create a thriving business with ROCEs close to 30 per cent.

In contrast, in a relatively dynamic industry—IT services—Infosys has struggled to adjust to the changes taking place in what its customers want, how they want it and how much they are willing to pay for it. As a result, Infosys' value levers (focus on solutions, focus on costs and build for SMAC) are largely the recipe for it to cope with a changing market whereas TTK Prestige's value levers (product innovation, distribution & supply chain management, top quality management) are the core drivers of its success over the past decade. The trick therefore is to understand how many different types of products a company manufactures, how it manufactures them and how it sells them. Associated with this is a flow of cash—from the time the company buys raw materials, to the time the goods leave its factory and until the point the company receives payment from its customer. Understanding this process—how a company generates cash and then re-invests it to generate even more cash—is at the heart of understanding a business model. Successful investors refuse to consider investing in companies where they cannot understand this process relatively easily.

For example, one of my clients, a fund manager in a mutual fund based in South India, refused to invest in gold finance companies through the entire 'gold mania' that swept across India from 2010–2013. Every six months I would meet him and ask him to consider investing in gold finance companies like Muthoot Finance and Mannapuram. Between December 2008 and December 2011 Mannapuram's share prices rose at a CAGR of 96 per cent as brokers such as myself impressed upon investors the huge reserves of gold that Indian households (especially those that don't have access to credit from the banking system) have and how easy it is for this segment of Indian society to borrow by offering this gold as collateral. However, my southern Indian client refused to buy into the notion saying that 'This feels like a bubble and I feel very uneasy if companies rally on the back of bubbles. I can't tell you exactly why I don't feel comfortable with these gold finance companies but I can't understand their runaway success and that makes me worry.'

Concerned by the rapid growth in the gold finance sector, in March 2012, the RBI announced that it would impose a ceiling on the loan-to-value (LTV) ratios at which these lenders could operate i.e. for every ₹100 of gold, the RBI wanted the lenders to provide only ₹60 of credit. Since the lenders were operating at LTVs close to 85 per cent rather than 60 per cent, their share prices fell by 50 per cent in the month following the RBI announcement. Then from September 2012 onwards, as it became clear that the US economy was emerging from its post-Lehman recession, gold prices started correcting. By

June 2013, gold prices, in US dollar terms, had fallen by 25 per cent from its September 2012 level. As gold prices started falling, brokers like myself started investigating how such a fall would impact the lenders. We found that even if a lender had lent at an LTV of 75 per cent, by the time the borrower was making his 'bullet' repayment a year hence, the effective LTV (adding the principal and the interest outstanding) was around 95 per cent. Now, if you further factored into this a fall in the price of gold of even 10 per cent, it was clear that the effective LTV was north of 100 per cent implying that the borrowers had no commercial incentive to repay. Not surprisingly therefore, between January and June 2013, as gold prices fell, the share prices of the gold financiers fell by another 50–70 per cent. I then ate humble pie and called up my client to commend him on his sagacity.

Rule 2: Only invest in companies which can generate cash flows and high return on capital employed (ROCE) for long periods of time.

'I look at the nature and the quality of the business. What kind of growth the environment will support—I don't believe in buying a company at replacement cost or things like that. I look at buying a share because of its growth potential. A related issue is of whether that growth will be profitable, what kind of ROCE can it sustain and for how long. What are the barriers to entry or the competitive advantages that the business enjoys which will support growth.'—Prashant Jain[4]

For as long as I have been a stockbroker, I have heard the same message from very successful long term investors—to generate market beating returns one needs to find franchises with sustainable competitive advantages which can generate cash flow

---

[4] *India's Money Monarchs*, Chetan Parikh, (Capitalideasonline.com, 2005), pg 165.

consistently and maintain a high ROCE for long periods of time. Let us delve into this powerful rule more deeply.

For a business to endure over long periods of time it needs to have sustainable competitive advantages. Since we discussed this concept in the previous chapter, I will only summarise it here. 'Sustainable competitive advantage' is what helps a firm ensure that the value that it adds is not easily eroded due to increasing competition or changing market conditions. Such advantages can come from two sources: distinctive capabilities or strategic assets. Strategic assets can be in the form of intellectual property (patents, proprietary knowhow), or legal rights (licenses, concessions) or in the form a natural monopoly. Distinctive capabilities are more intangible and can be grouped into three categories: (a) Brands and reputation; (b) Architecture (e.g. a network of specialised suppliers or a unique mentoring program for middle managers); and (c) Innovation.

> 'A really important characteristic that I look for is whether the business looks for cash over the medium term. I am convinced that cash-generating businesses are superior to the ones that consume cash...Businesses that can grow without requiring a lot of capital are particularly attractive. Cash-on-cash return is the ultimate measure of attractiveness in terms of valuation.'— Anthony Bolton[5]

Powerful competitive advantages allow a firm to generate cash flows on an ongoing basis. The reinvestment of the cash helps the firm, both, to expand and, ideally, to generate even more cash per unit sold. Whilst the former is self-explanatory (eg. a firm based in south India reinvests its profits and expands into northern India), the latter is more powerful. The latter would happen, say, when the same firm uses its cash flows to develop an even better product which can then be sold at a premium price. Long term investors therefore are always on the look-out for firms which can compound their cash flows in this fashion.

---

[5] *Investing Against the Tide*, Anthony Bolton, (FT Prentice Hall, 2009), pg 11.

'My investment philosophy is very simple. My objective is to invest in businesses that can generate superior return on capital over a period of time. I think this can primarily come out of intellectual capital mostly in terms of quality of management and depending on the businesses, [the] type of competitive advantages the management can build into a business.'—Sukumar Rajah[6]

Growth in profits or cash flow alone does not make a business valuable; you must investigate how much incremental capital was invested to generate this growth in profits. The financial ratio which allows you to track this dynamic is Return on Capital Employed (ROCE) i.e. 'profits after tax/capital employed' where capital employed is defined as the fixed assets used by the business e.g. plant and machinery) plus the working capital being used to finance the business. If this sounds too technical, there is another more intuitive way to understand ROCE. Over the long run if a business produces 15 per cent ROCE i.e. a 15 per cent return on the capital that it is investing, then that is the annual return you are likely to get from holding that stock.

It is worth remembering that even in a country with a high GDP growth rate, like India, businesses which generate healthy ROCEs over long periods of time are relatively rare. In fact, if you look at the twenty years to FY14, of the 5000-odd firms listed in India, only 79 firms (i.e. less than 2 per cent of the listed companies in India) have generated ROCEs of 15 per cent or more in at least eighteen of the last twenty years.

Generating healthy ROCEs over long periods of time is even harder than generating healthy cash flows because, even for a successful firm, every year the challenge is greater than the year before as the previous year's cash has to be invested sensibly. As the firm gets bigger, it has to find ways each year of successfully investing ever larger cash flows and very few businesses are able to pull this off over periods longer than five years.

---

[6] *India's Money Monarchs*, Chetan Parikh, (Capitalideasonline.com, 2005), pg 200.

The best example in India of a firm with superb cash flows but falling ROCEs is Infosys. Throughout the last twenty years Infosys has generated high levels of profitability (its operating margins have been nearly double that of its global peers such as Accenture and IBM) and hence strong cash flows. However, this firm has singularly failed to reinvest its surplus cash—net cash on Infosys' balance sheet as a multiple of shareholders' equity has risen from 0.47 times in FY03 to 0.59 times in FY13. As a result, Infosys' ROCE has fallen from 36 per cent in FY03 to 21 per cent in FY13. Over this period, Infosys' share price CAGR has been 19 per cent in Indian Rupee terms and 6 per cent in USD terms (ADR).

Over the same period both Accenture and IBM have continuously returned large doses of their surplus cash to shareholders (IT services, both in India and abroad, is a relatively capital-light business). Accenture's ROCE has risen from 69 per cent in FY03 to 72 per cent in FY13. IBM's ROCE has risen from 12 per cent in FY03 to 32 per cent in FY13. Over this period, Accenture and IBM's share prices have risen at a CAGR of 15 per cent and 8 per cent respectively in USD terms.

Rule 3: Buy the franchises identified by rule 2 when they are available at prices which build in a 'margin of safety'.

'I don't put a value on it but I look for significant buffers. I don't buy a company just because I think it's 20 per cent underpriced. I would look to buy a company which is 50–60 per cent undervalued because I could always make an error of 10–20 per cent in estimating the value of the company.'—Prashant Jain[7]

One aspect of successful long term investing is identifying companies which have sustainable competitive advantages, which generate cash flow and high ROCEs over long periods of time. But another, equally important aspect of the decision making process,

---

[7] *India's Money Monarchs*, Chetan Parikh, (Capitalideasonline.com, 2005), pg 166.

is to buy these franchises at the right prices. So what is the 'right price' for buying a successful company? The conventional textbook answer tends to be that you should buy a company if its share price is below the fair value of the stock. There are a variety of valid ways to calculate fair value. For example, the popular Discounted Cashflow (DCF) method wherein one forecasts the 'profit after tax plus depreciation, amortisation and other non-cash charges on the P&L minus maintenance capex and other non-cash credits on the P&L' and then discounts this using the cost of equity to estimate the fair value is one way. But, all methods offer us estimates. So regardless of whether I use the average P/E multiple at which the said company's listed competitors trade at or whether I use DCF or the Dividend Discount Model (wherein the forecast dividends of the company are discounted back using the cost of equity as the discount rate) to value the company, I am taking a stab in the dark in terms of estimating the value of the business. Leaving aside the possibility that my estimate of the fair value of the business could be inaccurate, there is also the problem that the share price may stay below its fair value for many years to come. As John Maynard Keynes memorably said 'There is nothing so disastrous as a rational investment policy in an irrational world.'

THE PRINCIPLE OF MARGIN OF SAFETY

In order to deal with these problems, the legendary American investor, Ben Graham came up with the concept of 'margin of safety' nearly 90 years ago. This school of investing says that not only should you buy stocks when they are trading in the market below their intrinsic value (or fair value), you should also seek a heavy discount to that fair value. Value investors from the Ben Graham school of investing seem to interpret this as at least a 10 per cent discount to fair value for high quality companies and as much as a 50 per cent discount for more speculative investments.

For example, if I were to take a well-established company like Maruti Suzuki, which has obviously powerful competitive advantages around brand, distribution and the largest 'after sales service' network in India, a 10–20 per cent fall in Maruti's share price on the back of, say, industrial unrest in Maruti's plants would prompt a value investor to take a long hard look at the company. On the other hand, for a company such as Crompton Greaves with less pronounced competitive advantages (particularly in its core power transmission and distribution business), a seasoned value investor would wait for a much bigger correction (around 50–70 per cent) before deciding to have a look at the business.

At a practical level, I interpret margin of safety to mean that you only buy the shares when the share price is at least 30 per cent below your estimate of fair value. In doing so you are cutting down the risk that: (a) your estimate of fair value is wrong; and (b) that you lose money on your investment as the stock market refuses to recognise your estimate of fair value. Successful investors specialise in recognising special situations where a fundamentally high quality company is trading way below its fair value due to exceptional reasons (a prolonged trade union strike, or a freak accident in its factory or a one-off drop in sales due to a transportation breakdown in a certain part of India). Successful investors use such windows of opportunity created by bad news to enter the market and buy big.

In August 2012 I saw a very effective demonstration of the margin of safety principle. As the Indian economy lurched downwards in FY12 and then into FY13, Maruti's share price fell sharply. The fall was compounded by its Japanese parent increasing the royalty rate it charges the company (from 3.5 per cent of sales to 5 per cent) and by labour problems in Maruti's plants near Delhi. Between 1 August 2010 and 18 July 2012, Maruti's share price fell by around 20 per cent. Then on the evening of 18 July 2012 during another trade union strike in Maruti's Manesar plant, violence broke out and one of Maruti's managers tragically lost his life. Maruti's share price fell by a further 12 per cent the end of the month. By the middle of August, Maruti's share price at ₹1,166 was firmly below our estimate of fair value and at 12 times forward earnings (i.e. the earnings that

Ambit's auto analyst expected Maruti to generate in the twelve months to March 2013) it was clearly an attractive investment given its well-known sustainable competitive advantages. The share price clearly had a margin of safety factored into it, I thought, but would anybody have the courage to buy given the perceived seriousness of the trade union dispute? In swooped a large British fund house and built a US$100mn position in the stock. Within six months, Maruti's share price had increased by 40 per cent.[8]

MEAN REVERSION

> *'Mean reversion is one of the great truisms of capitalism. For most companies, the financial statistics used to evaluate their performance, such as sales growth, margins or return on capital, revert to the mean over time. This also applies to valuations and, sometimes, even management's ability!'*—Anthony Bolton[8]

Seasoned investors are able to use a tried and tested 'thumb rule' in financial markets to time their investments effectively—mean reversion. Mean reversion refers to the systematic propensity of successful companies to slide towards mediocrity after an extended period of prosperity. My colleague, Gaurav Mehta, finds that nearly 85 per cent of successful Indian firms in the BSE500 slide to mediocrity (or worse) within five years of becoming what I would call a 'great' company i.e. a company which seems to be successful generating profits and cash flow and harvesting this capital for re-investment. Why do successful Indian businesses consistently damage themselves is one of the central areas of research for my colleagues.

Mean reversion also refers to the propensity of unsuccessful Indian firms to pick themselves and turn themselves around. Gaurav's work shows that nearly a third of Indian companies in the BSE500 move from being 'laggards' in their sector (i.e. amongst the worst 25 per cent of companies in a sector in terms

---

[8] *Investing Against the Tide*, Anthony Bolton, (FT Prentice Hall, 2009), pg 9.

of fundamental business performance) to leaders (i.e. amongst the best 25 per cent of companies in a sector) within a space of five years. This frequent transition from worst to best is another area of research that we are focusing on.

Just as we see mean reversion in underlying business performance, we also see the same feature in share prices. Great companies after a long upward run in share prices tend to start faltering in terms of successfully investing surplus capital. That drags ROCEs down and thus begins the downward slide in share prices. Great investors tend to be able to get out a few months before this decline begins. For example, another one of my clients based in southern India used to be a large holder of Infosys shares. In early 2011 he read a newspaper report that pay rises at Infosys were no longer higher than that of its peers. Worried that Infosys would end up losing its best people, he spoke to a few recruitment officers in universities based in South India. He found that Infosys was now hiring from the same campuses as all the other large IT services firms and offering the same salaries. That gave him an indication that Infosys' business performance would revert to the industry average (at that stage Infosys' operating margins were 300–400 basis points higher than those of its rivals). Hence he proceeded to sell his entire Infosys holding. In the year following his sale of Infosys shares, the share price fell by 20 per cent.

Similarly, mean reversion applies to the way in which we purchase stocks too—the rewards from investing in a firm which is almost on the verge of bankruptcy but then goes on to achieve great success can be huge. For example, TTK Prestige was listed in 1994 at a share price of ₹120. By 2003 TTK's share price had fallen to ₹7 and the company was considering becoming a 'sick' company. The company's management then pulled TTK back from the brink—they launched more products (beyond the traditional pressure cooker), expanded the company into northern India, dealt with their labour union issues, improved product quality and launched the Prestige Smart Kitchen chain of stores. Between June 2003 and June 2014, TTK Prestige's share price multiplied 500 times (or at a CAGR of 90 per cent)!

'EVEN MORE IMPORTANT THAN THE 'BUY DECISION IS HOW LONG YOU LET THAT POSITION RUN'

Akash Prakash *is the founder and CEO of Amansa Capital, a Singapore based foreign institutional investor. Prior to establishing Amansa Capital in 2006, Akash was Director of Investments (India) for Temasek Holdings, the investment vehicle of the government of Singapore. Before that Akash spent six years as a Portfolio Manager for GIC—The Government of Singapore Investment Corporation—where he managed US, Pan Asian and Indian investment portfolios. Akash also spent 6 years in the 1990s with Morgan Stanley where he was an Executive Director and Portfolio Manager of the Morgan Stanley Growth Fund. Morgan Stanley was one of India's largest foreign investors during this period. Akash has an MBA from IIM (Ahmedabad) and a Bachelor of Commerce from Bombay University.*

In your first buy-side avatar, in Morgan Stanley in the early 1990s, you were one of the first institutional investors to build and hold a 10 per cent + position in Infosys. What was the genesis of that investment?

AP: Our view has always been that we need to invest in companies where we can trust in the people who are running the company. Trust, in turn, is driven by capital allocation. Where you get shafted by entrepreneurs, other than through theft and bad accounting by crooks, is capital allocation. In an environment like India, where you always have so many 'perceived good opportunities', if you invest in poor capital allocators, you will never get a return. Other than returning it to you, poor capital allocators will always find something to do with your money. So our first rule for finding good investments is to find management teams who we trust.

Secondly, our firm belief is that good management teams create optionality for you in an environment like India, smart managers can create a lot of wealth. Therefore, even more important than the 'buy' decision, is how long you let that position run. To refer back to your example, at Morgan Stanley, at its peak, we owned 14 per cent of Infosys and I was responsible largely for that position. I don't think we deserve great credit for buying Infosys. What's creditworthy is that we held on to it for so long.

How did you manage to do that?

AP: Our view was clear that the company had immense opportunity, the growth runway was huge, the addressable market was incredible, the management team was phenomenal and the company had great governance. So we felt that, given the size of the addressable market and the quality of the management, even if the stock looks expensive on a short term basis, we should maintain our holding in this company. And I have to tell you that even in the 1990s, there were many points in time when Infosys looked expensive on a three or six months basis.

We see Eicher Motors as a similar case in point. We have a large position in Eicher. It is clearly expensive on a six-month basis. But the problem in India is that your impact cost of getting in and getting out a good midcap stock is very high. So we believe that if a company is well run and has a phenomenal three to four year opportunity, we have to hold the company through periods when the stock will not do much.

Are there specific 'selling rules' that you apply to your holdings?

AP: Unless a stock reaches an absurd valuation or if something fundamental has changed in the business environment for that company or something critical has changed in the company's growth outlook, we prefer not to sell stocks that we own. So taking Eicher as an example, clearly the commercial vehicle market is in the dumps at present because of the state of the economy. However, since we believe that the economy will recover in the not too distant future, since we can see Eicher consistently gaining market share and since we have faith in the management, we will continue holding the stock.

Our approach is to buy high quality companies and hold them for as long as we possibly can. Our view is that there are a limited number of companies in India where everything lines up; good business, capable and ethical management, you have access to the management. Such combinations do not come that often. So in situations like that, we like to ride the holding for as long as possible. I firmly believe in the gardening adage of 'grow your plants and take out the weeds'. What we try to do is have trigger rules which cut the losers and leave the winners intact.

Clearly, you have a well-defined approach to investing. Who were the people or what were the influences that helped you settle upon this approach?

AP: What helped initially was a lot of reading. I learnt a lot from two books by Robert Hagstrom called 'The Warren Buffett Way' and the 'Warren Buffett Portfolio'. The Warren Buffett portfolio talks exactly about this—have a concentrated portfolio of 14–30 stocks, know those stocks well and have low portfolio turnover. These books were instrumental in shaping my approach to investing. I learnt that risk is not volatility, risk is not standard deviation. Instead, risk is capital loss caused by the company you are buying.

We structured our investments based on this approach. If you look at our portfolio in Amansa that's how we started. If you look at our portfolio today we typically have 25 stocks. We are market cap agnostic. We have a typical holding period of three or four years. We try to know the companies as well as possible and our philosophy and approach is that if you invest in good businesses, they will reward you disproportionately over three or four years. To mitigate the very real risk of capital loss, you have to know your investee companies well, as well as you possibly can.

If you at look the Morgan Stanley Mutual Fund portfolio, when we began in the early 1990s, it was a classic mutual fund portfolio. 150 stocks, random, scattered investments. We did not know the companies well. Unsurprisingly, we did not do very well. We delivered a little above or little below what the market delivered. Then we went through a process of self-analysis. I realised that this was not the way to run money, especially not in the Morgan Stanley construct because you had locked in capital.

What you have to realise is that at Amansa now we have locked up stable capital, as was the case with Morgan Stanley then. I have tremendous respect for the Indian domestic mutual fund community because they have a very difficult job given they are managing money which comes in and goes out on a daily basis. In contrast to their reputation in the popular press, I think the mutual funds are smart investors who are dealing not just with peer group performance pressure but also uncertainty about the quantum of money they are managing. It is tough and yet if you look at the long term returns of the best mutual funds, they have done a good job. They are sometimes forced to do sub-optimal things because that is the nature of the construct they are forced to live with. They have to make short term calls, they have no choice as that's the nature of the beast.

That is why we have constructed Amansa very differently. We have consciously designed Amansa to be anti what the mutual funds are, to have the freedom to invest in a way that the mutual funds cannot. For example, if you look at our portfolio now, we have zero Hindustan Unilever, zero ITC, zero Glaxo Consumer. We don't have a single name in that sector. No mutual fund can invest like this. But the mutual funds have big holdings in these names, not because they believe that holding Hindustan Unilever at 40 times its earnings is a great idea, but because they can't take the business risk of not owning it. We can because we have constructed our portfolio in such a way that and we have constructed our investor base in such a way that they understand what we are trying to do. Obviously, we could be wrong but our bet is that having taken the pain, it would be silly to buy Hindustan Unilever at this valuation.

Given your investing style, my guess is that in years like 2006 and 2007, you would have had to deal with underperformance. How did you manage that?

AP: We were lucky to be underperforming by 3-4 per cent in a year with a massive absolute performance. In fact, in 2007 we had a monster year in terms of absolute performance. The market was up 70 per cent and we were up 67 per cent. Smart investors are forgiving about such underperformance because they have seen such patterns before. In fact, the smart LP base understands that in monster years for the market, we will underperform. (LPs are the "limited partners" who invest in a fund.) They know that our type of strategy should hold up very well when economic growth goes down. In 2008, when the market tumbled downwards, we went down as well but less than the market did. Our style will do much better, relative to the market, in a year in which the market is up 10–15 per cent.

We recognise that as an investor you will go through phases of underperformance. Just look at Warren Buffett's group of dozen or so close friends who are almost all legendary investors and disciples of Graham and Dodd. Except Buffet, every one of these investors has been through periods of underperformance stretching over 3–4 years. And that is the dilemma of fund management. If you are going to evaluate someone on the basis of one, two or three year performance, how do you separate random chance from skill? It's a fundamental problem because the best, smartest investors can have two very bad years. I would argue that in a twenty year career in investment management, you are likely to have a long period of underperformance. So unless you have a realistic perspective regarding your investment performance, unless you give yourself the chance to sit back and think rationally about investing, it is very difficult to perform.

There are many sectors in India where successful investing seems to involve backing promoters who get along with politicians. How do you assess such promoters from a 'management quality' perspective?

AP: First of all, we avoid sectors which have massive government interference. We don't invest in infrastructure and property by and large. We don't invest in natural resources by and large.

Then there are other sectors where there is some government involvement; that level of government involvement you can't get away but the bet you are making is that the promoter is an honest person. He only takes out of the company what is required for business purposes and for managing the environment but he does not take out more than that.

Now let's take a situation like Infosys where the management team is ethical and capable but, arguably, the sector and perhaps the company is structurally challenged. How do you make an investment call in a situation like that?

AP: The investment call on Infosys is a very interesting call today because the market is slowly giving up on the company. Although it is still a very good business, the market is saying that they have lost the plot. Now is this a short term cyclical problem or is this a much deeper structural problem? The answer to that question is still not obvious. We are trying to make up our mind on this. Ultimately it is a judgement call. There is no hard and fast metric on this. They clearly have gone through management issues and churn. The only way we can understand is by meeting management, meeting competitors, talking to customers. However, one needs to remember that with a company like Infosys, if it becomes cheap enough, the downside becomes low. Then the risk:reward ratio is in your favour such that even if you are wrong, your chances of capital loss are low. You will lose at best 5–10 per cent.

Clearly then valuation plays a role in your buying decision?

AP: It does play a role. We don't buy momentum stocks trading at 40 times earnings. We don't buy concept stocks. Yes, that means that we will miss a few stocks like Jubilant Foodworks but we will also avoid five mistakes. Our view is that the burden of expectation is too high. Something will go wrong in one quarter and the stock will be down 30 per cent. When we are entering a stock, it should not be trading at anything more than 15–20 times earnings. Ideally, we want to buy at 10–12 times earnings.

How do you deal with the sheer amount of 'noise' in the Indian market? Broker notes, brokers' phone calls, management commentary…how do you deal with it?

AP: Being in Singapore helps. Sitting in India the noise is that much greater because it is that much easier for people to bombard you with stuff. Secondly, I don't take phone calls. This may be perceived as being arrogant but I don't like spending time on the phone. Thirdly, even with regards to email traffic, I don't think I read more than 15–20 emails a day. Finally, I don't keep a Bloomberg terminal on my desk; it is kept outside the office. As you can see, we have been sitting and chatting for an hour and I have not received one phone call.

How do you build conviction in an investment without that conviction turning into confirmation bias?

AP: That is a tough one because that is a classic dilemma. What we try to do is be as open minded as possible and encourage debate in the office as much as possible. There are five of us in the team. Before we buy anything, we have multiple discussions and everyone is encouraged to disagree and debate. We have a group meeting every day. Before we build a sizeable position, we build our own financial model of the company. Before we make the final investment decision in Singapore, that financial model is circulated to all five of us and then we sit down and debate the decision based on the financial model. We discuss what is the thesis, why are we buying this stock, what is the upside and what are the risks. People are free to disagree. They can poke holes in the investment thesis or the financial model. I think that's the only way to do it. And our people are comfortable saying 'I don't agree'. Sometimes I am the only guy saying that 'we should buy this stock' and the other four say that 'no, this is too risky'.

Take Sun TV as a case in point. I think it is an outstanding business. However, there are other factors, which the team said make it a risky business including the fact that it is has to contend with a public sector cable operator in Tamil Nadu. We bought Sun TV when it was at 10 times earnings and giving a 6 per cent dividend yield and had outstanding cash metrics. Yes, there were risks around litigation but none of cases were against Sun TV and at those valuations, we felt it was worth buying. All of that being said, we were cognizant of the risks of the position and hence did not bet the house on it.

The five of you discuss your portfolio every week?

AP: Not every stock. We discuss the ones where there have been material developments, say a change in management or say, results coming in weaker than expected. Then we ask ourselves whether, in light of the developments, our view of the company has fundamentally changed. If it has, should we buy more or should we sell.

You have been investing for 20 years now of which the last seven years have been at Amansa. Does the job get easier as the years go by?

AP: In some ways it does get easier over time because as you get more experience, hopefully you avoid the more routine mistakes. I hopefully wouldn't get tempted by some random company today that looks cheap. I won't even spend even one minute thinking about it because my investment framework is now clear in my mind. Therefore, in that sense in this industry you do get better with experience. You have more points of comparison and you learn as the years go by. Secondly, as you get older and your investment framework and philosophy becomes more clearly defined, you have more clarity about what you want to invest in. In effect, you become more rigid in your framework and that helps you cross out a lot of substandard investment opportunities. On the other hand, it is also the case that as you get older, you become slower at absorbing information and the amount of information you can hold in your mind reduces. I could remember the details of balance sheets far more easily twenty years ago than I can do now. I could tell you off the top of my head, the shares outstanding for most companies.

Ultimately, however, the enjoyment for people like us is finding a good company early even before the market starts talking about it, identifying a good management team and seeing the company grow. That enjoyment is undiminished over time. I believe that there are two types of investors. Those who like the thrill of investing, they want to be right and they enjoy the thrill of the intellectual challenge being early investors in a company. They like identifying the company, betting on good management and then seeing the stock go up five times. Such investors enjoy the intellectual kick one gets from being right. It is the thrill of the chase in a way or rather the intellectual satisfaction of being ahead of the curve. The second kind is those who are more driven by scale. These guys want to manage many billions of dollars and be the most powerful investors in the market. There is nothing wrong with that. It is a different style and I have to admit there is a kick from being one of the biggest investors in town. I did that 10–20 years ago. So having been there and done that, that no longer has any attraction for me.

So will Amansa consciously avoid becoming a big fund?

AP: Yes, we are very clear that we will never becoming a giant fund. We will not cross a US$1 billion and we have told our investors that. Once you cross that threshold, it becomes harder to perform. You can't have a 25-stock portfolio and manage US$4 billion. It is not possible.

We are very clear that we are not trying to be the largest fund management house in India. We are very clear that we are going to manage money of a particular style and type and I will take my time to build that kind of investor base. It can be done but one needs to be patient and spend two or three years. When we began Amansa seven years ago, we only started with US$25 million. We could have got a lot more money quickly had we accepted money without lock-ups but we made a conscious decision that we don't want hot money which flies in and out quickly. We want long term, stable capital. It will take far longer to build but hopefully it will be far stickier and will stay longer. Long term investors do a lot more diligence on the funds that they put money into. They also look for a longer track record before they commit their capital. As a result in the initial years, we grew slowly and gradually. So it is a call one has to make—do you want to make a quick buck or are you in it for 5–10 years. We are clear about where we stand on that issue.

'I COULD FEEL THE BUBBLE IN 2007'

Sankaran Naren *is the CIO of ICICI Prudential Mutual Fund, his first and, to date, only employer in the investment management profession. Educated at IIT (Chennai) and IIM (Kolkata), he started investing money during his school days. By the time, Naren joined ICICI Prudential as a fund manager in 2004, he had been investing in the stock market for nearly 15 years. As the CIO one of the largest equity asset management houses in India and as a fund manager of some of the largest funds in the country, Naren now has a decade's worth of experience of how to deal with the extreme pressures of investing public money in front of the arc lights of the financial community.*

How did you first get involved with the stock market?

N: I was an only child. I lost my mother when I was 14. So what happened was that we were a two person household—my father and I—from the time I was 14.

SM: This was in Chennai?

N: Yeah. My father was a small investor who started investing during the FERA (Foreign Exchange Regulations Act) driven dilutions of the seventies. And one of the points that my father and I talked about was the stock market. As you might know, in the seventies the Indian stock market was like a lottery. The FERA dilutions resulted in all the MNCs getting listed in India and we bought them at IPOs. The allotment was like a lottery and then you made money like a lottery. That's how it all started and I enjoyed the whole process. But then somehow by luck I got admission into IIT where I studied engineering. I had no interest in the area. I possibly had more aptitude in Maths than in engineering but the entrance examination is a test of aptitude in mathematics and science so somehow I got a place in IIT. Because I knew what I wanted to do, I landed up in IIM immediately after graduation. I specialised in Finance.

Surely, in those days it must have been unusual for someone from Chennai to be interested in markets and finance. Were you not very different from your peer group?

N: Yeah. I used to play a lot of bridge those days in IIT and I was known as possibly one of the few people interested in the stock markets. Remember, in those days making any money was difficult. So the fact that my father and I were making money from investing in stocks sustained my interest. Our strategy was to invest in a public issue and then sell our allotments. I would be advising him on which IPOs to pick up.

In those pre-Internet days, how did you assess the quality of these public issues?

N: It was very rudimentary knowledge if you ask me. I knew the products that they were making rather than knowing whether their EPS figure was good or bad. In the 1980s, it was like a lottery. I accepted that. And then after joining IIM, over a period of time I learnt how to read annual reports. In the 1980s, the number of people who knew how to read annual reports were very few. Most chartered accountants were more interested in making annual reports than reading them. So eventually in 1989 when I graduated from IIM, I tried to get into SBI Caps which was the mecca of finance at that time. Instead I joined ICICI which was the other mecca. Those were the two meccas at the time.

During my stint at ICICI, I learnt project appraisal which was the closest thing to equity research at that time. In 1989 when I left IIM and came to Chennai, one stock I looked at was LMW (Lakshmi Machine Works). It was trading at that point of time at price to earnings of 2x, price to cash earnings of 1x and they had a four-year order book. So you can imagine how inefficient the market was. There used to be a Madras Stock Exchange. I went to meet one of the broking firms on the stock exchange and asked them what they thought of LMW. The broker said that no one has made any money investing in a Coimbatore-based company. LMW then went up 30 fold in the period between 1989 and 1994.

By this time you had opened your own broking account presumably?

N: Actually I still traded on my father's money. It was a still a two member household and two people earning income in 1989. I managed to convince my father that it was time to move out of the primary market into the secondary market. And I convinced him to remove the debt portion of our asset allocation completely because we had become a two-income, two-member household and hence could take more risk.

At that point did you try to assess how much money you had made in the preceding five years?

N: No nothing like that at all. We were trying to do small cap investing. In 1989–1990, stocks were trading at price to earnings multiples of 1x, 2x, 3x. Some stocks were even trading below earnings! In 1990 I quit project financing at ICICI and joined HSBC. ICICI had taught me how to analyse a company before signing off on a long term loan. From 1990–1994 I was an investment banker at HSBC. We were primarily doing public issues out of HSBC's Chennai office and in those years we had the tough job of dealing with the Controller of Capital Issues (CCI). Then public issue pricing was liberalised and you immediately moved out of the model where the public issue was a lottery. With CCI pricing removed, we as investment bankers had to take a decision on pricing. From 1990–1994, as you know, we saw a superb rally. Then there was a crisis [the one triggered by Harshad Mehta] but since we were long term investors we did nothing.

By 1994 I thought I knew stock market investing because of the multi-baggers that I had made between 1989 and 1994. Then 1994–1996 turned out to be very testing years. Once you have had a thirty bagger [i.e. a stock which goes up 30 fold], inevitably if you are an equity investor you'll get drunk and you make a set of mistakes. These mistakes pushed our portfolio into very bad shape by 1996. We lost a lot of money because I had not realised that what had happened between 1989 and 1994 was a one-time event. Basically we had reaped in those years the fruits of liberalisation and we were lucky to be in the right place at the right time. Then I joined a Chennai based broking firm in 1994 and became a stockbroker. The 1989–1994 euphoria meant that by 1996 I had made mistakes. Then in 1996, when I realised that instead of stars, my holdings had become dogs, there was a nice group set up in Chennai which I became a part of. These were essentially people who understood equities and wanted to share their mistakes.

How many people were in that group?

N: About seven or eight. I happened to go even last Saturday to Chennai to talk to the people in that group. It has grown from eight to eighteen Chennai based investors. There is a person called Kamal Chaddha who has been the coordinator from 1996 to now. And I got a chance last Saturday to meet them again and we had dinner. Anyhow 1996 began the phase when we started learning from the mistakes we had made. We then shared our mistakes openly with each other. Today in retrospect, I can say that my discussions with this group created a framework for investing and that framework from 1996–1997 helped all of us in that group stay out of the tech bubble.

So this was the first time you created an investment framework?

N: It wasn't just me, the group created the framework together. The key test of a framework is whether it helps identify a bubble.

Can you help me understand the framework?

N: Intuitively, in retrospect I can say that we understood that there would be something called an investment cycle and that there would be a period where some people would get overexcited. In those days the only way we could figure out this period of over-excitement was to look at a quantitative kind of model where you looked at price to earnings. In 1999–2000 we could see that a number of stocks traded at very high price to earnings (PE). We were very negative on the 100 PE companies and we watched 60 PE becoming 80 PE becoming 100 and then

120-150. And then you had the 5-10 PE companies remaining exactly where they were. You had a situation which was very frustrating. But the basic test of an investor is how you handle a bubble and whether you are capable of staying rational. That's what we did in 1999-2000.

That must have been difficult given how all pervasive the media promotion of that bubble was.

N: Yes. And that's why the group exists until now because you need psychological support when you are stuck. You are not interested in challenging the market but you wanted to stay in the zone of what you thought you wanted to do. 1999-2000 was amazing and after that when the bubble burst I was in Mumbai and I was in HDFC Securities. By the time the market crashed in 2001, I was Vice President (Operations) at HDFC Securities. That was my first job in Mumbai. In 2001-2002 I realised that people had lost faith in equities. I realised that I had research capabilities and my boss asked me to become Head of Research in addition to my responsibilities as VP (Operations).

In those days I used to go to my friends and tell them that the market looks dirt cheap and that you should put all your money in the market—sell your house and put your money in the market. You should have nothing called fixed deposits, you should leverage and invest in the market. At the time people were not willing to listen. Then 2003 happened and markets started to move up. But no one in India benefited because only the FIIs bought. By that time I wanted to be in a full time research role. I didn't want to be in Operations. So I moved into the role of Head of Institutional Equities at Refco [which went on to become MF Global after Refco collapsed].

To be honest, I had come to Mumbai with the intention of being a fund manager. Then thanks to a few friends, ICICI Prudential Mutual Fund hired me. Nilesh Shah, the then CIO, recruited me. I was given ₹180 crore across two funds to manage in 2004. I was given ₹130 crore in a fund called Discovery and ₹50 crore in a smaller tax saving fund. That's how I started in fund management. After that 2007 was again a very tough year.

Why was 2007 a tough year?

N: In addition to my underperformance as a fund manager, my son then seven years old was diagnosed with having a learning disorder. This was a very difficult time which was brilliantly handled by my wife with great maturity. In 2010, we later discovered that the reason for the learning disorder was that my son had a rare genetic disorder called Fragile X disorder. My wife and I have become subject matter experts on the disorder and have worked to creating a resource base in India for the disorder.

I had been trained to be cautious in bubbles. In my experience of having got burnt in 1995 and having avoided 2000, I could feel the bubble in 2007. So my two funds (Dynamic and Discovery) underperformed the benchmark by 15 per cent in 2007.

How did you deal with underperformance?

N: There were divergent views at that point in time within our investments team and it was very challenging. The investment group in Chennai also helped as they were more accustomed to handling bubbles. I would say 2007 was a very difficult year but I was lucky because I also managed an infrastructure fund where by virtue of the mandate the fund gave phenomenal returns without buying the low quality power utility and construction stocks.

How did you achieve that—giving returns comparable to the infrastructure stocks without buying infra stocks?

N: Because I had lot of experience in metals, we made a lot of money buying metals. So instead of getting into power utilities and construction we bought metals. In 2007 metals also did well. But by the end of 2007 even metal stocks started getting frothy.

Between 2006 and 2009 the infrastructure story that was sold to investors was that India needs so much infrastructure that it does not matter what valuation multiple an infrastructure company was trading at, it would go up. How did you avoid succumbing to that story?

N: I find the trailing PE a very useful multiple. Even in 2007, the trailing PE of any capital goods company was frightening because it was around 50. Given my experiences in the 1990s, whenever I see trailing PEs of more than 40, a big red light is switched on in my head. So in that sense spotting the infra bubble in 2007 was, in cricketing terms, a "sitter".

If I look at your investing behaviour over time, as your knowledge is going up, your conviction is growing in parallel. You have moved from buying public issues to buying secondary, from advising family and friends to advising clients, from doing sell-side research to becoming a fund manager. If you look at the past 20 years, what are the other experiences which have really influenced your behaviour— books, courses, people, stocks?

N: In the 1980s and 1990s to be honest, Warren Buffet was the person you read to understand investing. I didn't have access to institutional research until I joined ICICI as fund manager. So today I would say I have three gurus: Michael Mauboussin, Howard Marks and James Montier. In those days the gurus were not clear in my mind. In 2000 and upto 2007 the advantage was that you could have bought Buffet's stocks because they were cheap. But it was very evident in 2007 that something was going drastically wrong in the stock market. It was very hard to deal with and this is the biggest problem of being a good equity investor: he will look like an idiot at times and he must know how to handle that.

So it was interesting that I was running a fund that was underperforming the benchmark and I was also running the best performing infra fund. But it was very challenging for me to keep my valuation thesis intact. That is where I guess experience helps. The ability to say that 'I will look like a fool but in the short run looking like a fool doesn't worry me'.

So do you think it is possible for an investor to 'anchor' himself and thus prevent himself from being dragged around by greed and fear?

N: I don't believe that it is possible for one person without the psychological support of others around him to be able to handle a bubble.

By 2007 how would you describe your investment approach—value oriented or growth oriented?

N: In 2007 I went through one phase which was very depressing. As it is, I was a low price to book, low PE investor and an anti-high PE investor. But somewhere in 2007 in my value fund I had a few textile, fertiliser and paper companies and I felt very bad that I had violated the Warren Buffet rules. Buffet clearly says that beyond valuation multiples, you have to look at the quality of the business also whereas I was too fascinated by the low price to book and low PE multiples. That was very irritating.

I found that the pharma sector in 2007 had low PEs and good business. I put that in my value fund and in my dynamic fund. I found stocks like Cadilla, low profile companies like FDC and some MNC pharma names. And after that I decided to not only look at low PE multiples but also look at the quality of businesses that I was investing in. But if you ask me, in my genes I still try to buy some low price to book, low PE stocks of average businesses. That is in my genes and that has been my investment argument since the 1980s. 2007 was the first time I realised that I had made a blunder and I had to reorient and say that you need to look at RoE, ROCE, etc.

Let's now discuss the Lehman-bust in 2008 and the aftermath in 2009. How were those two years for you?

N: There are certain things I am happy about. In 2008 after Lehman collapsed, I went to many cities of India and told them that there is sale in equities going on. If you have discount sale in Westside, you buy clothes, in Landmark you buy books; now you have a discount sale in equities and none of you are buying.

This was a common statement I made in many parts of India and that I am happy about. But if you see 2009 what I am unhappy about is that I was managing four funds at the time—Discovery, Dynamic, Infrastructure and Tax—and what I did was I was used to write call options [i.e. sell call options] as a way of reducing the risk of a fund. I continued with that strategy for Dynamic and Infrastructure in 2009 as well. They suffered a lot especially in May 2009 when the general elections happened and the market soared.

In Discovery and Tax which were small and mid-cap funds I didn't write these call options and I was basically invested in these stocks. In 2009 these were the best performing funds in their categories—tax and mid cap categories. I was bought into the cheap stocks and basically fully invested. So I could have handled Dynamic and Infrastructure better had I not written those call options. I should have had a fully invested portfolio in all my funds. I knew that the market was cheap. I did tell everyone that the market was cheap so why did I write call options? This was something I asked myself and felt bad.

Once 2009 happened and I read all the new gurus (Montier, Marks and Mauboussin) it became very clear that the way forward is to be counter cyclical and to watch cycles and sentiments of investors closely. So in 2009 Dynamic had a model of being conservative...we created a good model which allowed us to be counter cyclical—as the market goes up, I increase my cash holdings and as the market goes down, I decrease my cash holdings. In 2010 we had 35 per cent cash and in December 2011 we had almost no cash (5–6 per cent) in the fund. Now that we have developed this model, the fund has outperformed its benchmark through 2009–2012. We have a clear counter cyclical model which I apply in many sectors. That model is working properly and I have not had a consumer stock in my portfolio in the last few quarters because my high trailing PE filter comes in.

Howard Marks talks about the many ways of trying to judge a cycle. Other than PE and market exuberance, what other indicators do you use to judge a cycle?

N: See for me what works is the market cap of the star company of the time. In 2000, my group in Chennai noted that it was illogical that Infosys was worth more than the market cap of the steel and cement sector. In 2007 we noted that the market cap of DLF was greater than that of the entire healthcare sector. You can use these multiples to sanity check the valuations of specific star stocks and hence identify where we are in the cycle.

Post 2008–2009 Nilesh Shah gave me the job of looking at investment strategy and the economy and I have found the entire experience of the last five years extremely fascinating. For instance, we at ICICI realised in 2009 that India has a problem with its current account deficit (CAD). We have had large overweights on exporters since then. That being said, my experience of top down investing has not been that great. For example, on 1 January 2012 I thought that with a high CAD likely for India, technology stocks would do very well. But in 2012 technology was the worst performer. In the second half of 2013 our top down processes have worked like a breeze as we have been overweight IT, overweight exporters and underweight consumer.

What I have learnt is that it is not essential that one particular thought of yours will work for you all the time. You have to at a particular point of time judge the situation and balance your top down and bottom-up processes. So for example, another way of trying to assess whether a sector is cheap or not is by looking at the weightage in the index over a period of time. So if I see a very large weightage for a sector then intuitively I am a bit cautious about the sector. Banks today would fall in that bucket. Similarly if you go back to 2007 when telecom had become 10 per cent of the benchmark, I used to tell people that telecom looks overvalued. So if you ask me, market cap and sector weightages in the large cap index have been good guides to where we are in the cycle.

How do you stay consistent to these 'rules of thumb'?

N: Once we settle upon a thumb rule, I let everybody in the company know about and I talk to my clients incessantly about it in our conference calls. I have realised that all rules of thumb are powerful only if you realise that you will be right perhaps only for a minority of the time but in those few weeks, you will generate the majority of your outperformance.

So by articulating your thumb rules to everyone around you, you are helping yourself pre-commit to the thumb rules?

N: Yes and it also helps me because my job is managing public money and because these kinds of rules are known to all my colleagues, they will come and tell me if I am deviating. It pre-commits my behaviour and that's important when I am under stress. There is another way for you to stay consistent to your own investing style and that is to have a group of colleagues who you have known for a long period of time, whose investing style you understand and who, in turn, understand your investing style.

I became the CIO of ICICI Prudential Mutual Fund in 2011. Between 2004 and 2007 we had added a number of experienced people. I found that the investing processes of several of these people were clashing with each other. As I thought things through, I felt it was better to have internally grown people. So we stopped recruitment of seasoned professionals. We have lost four seasoned investment professionals in recent years but we have not hired from outside. We have replaced the exiting team members with internal people. As a result, I know each person's strengths and weaknesses. For example, I am value contra investor but my colleague, Manish Gunwani, is a growth investor and Yogesh Bhatt, another fund manager in my team, is more of a benchmark-oriented guy. So we are able to use each other's strengths to strengthen our internally created top down and bottom-up investment processes.

A by-product of this approach to investing is that our assets under management are much more spread across half a dozen or so fund managers instead of being concentrated in my hands. We want to be a large fund management house, not a boutique. To become large without compromising clients' interests, we needed to create investment management expertise across the team without compromising on quality or performance. In that regard, I think we have made a lot of progress.

Anything else you would like to add?

N: I hope that value investing is more recognised as a good investment technique in India as it is in the West. I also hope that we at ICICI Prudential Asset Management Company continue to be regarded as a good investment house for the public money we manage. On a personal note, I hope that a cure is found in my lifetime for my son's genetic disorder, Fragile X.

FOUR

The Contrarian Mind

'[My] central principal of investment is to go contrary to the general opinion, on the grounds that if everyone agreed about its merit, the investment is inevitably too dear and therefore unattractive.'—John Maynard Keynes[1]

It was raining hard in Mumbai in August 2013 and the rupee was sliding as fast as the raindrops down my office window—from around ₹54 per US dollar in the middle of May 2013, it had fallen to around ₹63 per US dollar by 19 August 2013. Global investors, already worried on account of India's soaring current account deficit (which exceeded 5 per cent of GDP in the year to March 2013 from its typical levels over the preceding decade of around 2 per cent of GDP), had been spooked by the Federal Reserve Chairman Ben Bernanke's statement made on 19 June 2013 that the Fed was considering gradually unwinding the unprecedented wave of cheap liquidity, which it had unleashed on the global financial system to help America recover from the Great Financial Crisis of 2008. With the RBI and the Finance Ministry seemingly

---

[1] *Investing Against the Tide*, Anthony Bolton, (FT Prentice Hall, 2009), pg 39.

helpless, billions of dollars of Indian debt had been sold by foreign institutional investors (FIIs) in the two months following this fateful speech.

As the rupee sank, the Sensex fell from 20,150 on 19 June 2013 to 18,300 by 19 August; a 9 per cent decline. Financial Services companies' share prices, always highly sensitive to perceptions regarding the Indian economy's robustness, fell by almost twice as much the Sensex. In particular, IDFC, a well-managed non-bank lender, focusing on the Indian infrastructure sector saw its share price fall by 30 per cent from ₹144 on 19 June to ₹101 by 19 August.

In the midst of this meltdown in IDFC's share price one of the largest FIIs investing in India, at that time, bought as much IDFC stock as could be found in the market. This was also a time when confidence regarding India was at its lowest since the Lehman meltdown of September 2008, *The Economist* published an in-depth piece titled *'How India got its funk?'* (24 August 2013). It summarised the situation nicely by saying:

'Not so long ago India was celebrated as an economic miracle. In 2008, Manmohan Singh, the prime minister, said growth of 8–9 per cent was India's new cruising speed. He even predicted the end of the "chronic poverty, ignorance and disease, which has been the fate of millions of our countrymen for centuries". Today he admits the outlook is difficult. The rupee has tumbled by 13 per cent in three months. The stock market is down by a quarter in dollar terms. Borrowing rates are at levels last seen after Lehman Brothers' demise. Bank shares have sunk.'

Throughout the week commencing 19 August 2013, IDFC's share price continued to fall and every morning the FII in question asked its brokers to buy as much IDFC stock as could be found in the market. By the close of 22 August this investor had bought over 5 per cent of IDFC's shares outstanding (which amounted to a position significantly in excess of US$100 million). IDFC's management, which had plans of becoming a bank, realised that an FII holding more than 5 per cent of its stock could be an issue. The RBI does not approve of any party owning more than

5 per cent of shares outstanding in a bank. It then passed a Board resolution on 23 August 2013 which, in effect, prohibited FIIs from buying any more IDFC shares. This cap bought the FII's buying in IDFC shares to an end on 23 August. That day IDFC's share price was ₹103. As I write this chapter in late-August 2014, IDFC's share price has recovered to ₹150, up nearly 50 per cent since the preceding August

The FII in question had done its research on IDFC more than eight months before the purchase. In the early months of 2013, when the investor was studying IDFC, the company's share price was ₹180. The investor knew that IDFC was a well-managed lender and hence worthy of being part of his portfolio. But he also knew that the stock would struggle to earn a return if he purchased the company at 1.5 times its book value (which was what ₹180 translated into). So he waited for IDFC's share price to crack and when it cracked, due to the Fed's announcement of 'tapering', the FII entered the market and bought big at around ₹100 (translating into 0.7 times its book value).

Every other month or so I get to see one or two episodes like this—when a seasoned investor takes a decision that most ordinary investors would not imagine taking, either buying big when nobody else is doing so or selling a stock when the market is singing its praises. This ability to think differently is a trait of all great investors and the good news is that this ability can be acquired. The basic ingredients that nurture this trait have been listed in the previous chapters. In this chapter I will provide the mental mindset which allows the Gurus of Chaos to catalyse all of these ingredients—the 10,000 hours of practice, their knowledge of sustainable competitive advantages, of accounting and of promoter integrity—together with straightforward rules for decision making into market beating investment decisions.

My personal experience of training new analysts in Ambit Capital and watching young analysts in investment firms learn the trade and gradually grow into successful fund managers is that to build the mindset to successfully invest for the long run one has to follow a certain behavioural sequence. The first step in that sequence is to learn to control your 'reflex' brain or, to put it more crudely, your animal instincts. This is a major stepping stone, the foundation as it were of a series of traits which are usually the hallmarks of successful long-term investors, namely: risk aversion, openness to new information and concepts, patience, preparation and the intellectual courage to disagree with broader market opinion. Assiduous cultivation of these traits, especially the final trait—contrarianism—over long periods of time allows investors to conquer fear and greed, the two primal emotions that plague the rest of us.

Before we begin exploring these traits, one caveat. Over the last decade a number of insightful books have been written on behavioural finance by psychologists. My favourites from a long list are *Thinking Fast and Slow* by the Nobel laureate Daniel Kahneman, *Your Money and Your Brain* by Jason Zweig, *Quiet: The hidden power of introverts* by Susan Cain and *Think Twice* by Michael Mauboussin. Since I have no training as a psychologist, this chapter contains my interpretation—in light of my personal experiences—of what these experts are seeking to tell the world.

CONTROLLING THE "REFLEX" BRAIN

As articulated by Daniel Kahneman, our brain has two parts:
- the reflex brain which helps us deal with external stimuli and react instinctively in the most effective manner possible, and
- the more thoughtful reflective brain which helps us think, analyse, calculate and make intelligent, often complex, decisions.

Evolution has given all of us a powerful reflex brain which can help us deal with complex stimuli in an instinctive manner. So for example, whilst crossing the street, we are, almost effortlessly, gauging the distance and speed of other vehicles, assessing the movements of other pedestrians, inspecting the surface quality of the road (especially important in Mumbai) and calibrating our movements accordingly. Similarly, when a cricket ball is thrown, the fielder instinctively gauges its flight, speed and trajectory and positions his hands accordingly. However, this reflex brain can get us into trouble especially when it overrides the more reflective side of our brain.

My first experience of what can go wrong when the reflexive brain gets in the way of its reflective cousin took place in my school's cricket ground. As a 15 year old, I used to be a leg spin bowler for my school's junior cricket team. Since our school had a small cricket ground, the coach had specifically spent hours instructing me on how to slow down my bowling if the batsman started whacking me around. Bowling slower and flighting the ball more improved my chances of turning the ball sharply and thus making it harder for a batsman to hit me. I understood this basic principal of spin bowling well and become keenly aware of its efficacy while watching cricket on TV. Then came the day of the big match. By the time the ball had been handed to me, my adrenal glands were firing all cylinders and my mouth was dry. My reflexive brain overpowered its reflective side and ignoring all the training that had been imparted to me, I tried to zip the ball in as quick as I could. My first over went for 18 runs and my second one went for 16. With that my nascent cricketing career came to a premature end. Away from the comfort of the nets and practice matches, I simply could not heed my training when faced with the pressure of a real cricket match.

Says the University of Oregon psychologist, Paul Slovic, *'The reflexive system is very sophisticated and has served us well for millions of years. But in a modern world, where life is full of much more complicated problems than just immediate threats, it's not adequate and is likely to get us into trouble."* In the context of investing, this override—by the reflexive brain of the reflective brain—becomes particularly troublesome in four specific types of circumstances.

Trap 1: What you see is all there is (WYSIATI)

Our intuitive mind is designed to think fast, suppress doubt and make sense of partial information in a complex world. Furthermore, much of the time the coherent story it pulls together is close enough to reality to support reasonable action. In fact, our minds are built in such a way that neither the quality nor the quantity of evidence that we have impacts the action that we are taking (due to our beliefs). We often fail to allow for the possibility that evidence that should be critical to our judgement is missing—what we see is all there is ('WYSIATI' is Daniel Kahneman's acronym for this).

A common example of this is investors' desire to buy stocks in fast growing sectors. In the bull market which began in March 2009, investors were so swayed by India's rapidly growing demand for power that in the space of six months, they purchased nearly US\$3 billion of shares issued by newly created power utility companies. Very few investors bothered asking whether these utility companies had access to coal, or any experience of managing power plants, or indeed a reliable set of financial statements. All of these were taken as a given as investors piled into the power utilities' IPOs and QIPs.

Trap 2: Anchoring and Priming

Psychologists have highlighted how easy it is for even rational people to get 'anchored' and 'primed' by even random data. The manner in which one chooses to present statistical patterns influences people's responses. For instance if we were to conduct a survey and ask people to guess: 'How old was Mahatma Gandhi when he was assassinated?' and: 'Was Mahatma Gandhi more than 130 years old when he was assassinated?'—the answer to the latter question would get a significantly better response than the former. Reason: The figure 130, nonsensical as it is, offers an anchor and thus primes respondents to give a higher answer.

Similarly, daily negative news about the state of the Indian economy (corruption scandals, power blackouts, accounting scandals, profit warnings etc.) is likely to drag down people's growth and valuation estimates for all things Indian. Before you know it, you will be mentally trapped into undervaluing good Indian companies.

My favorite stock in this context is Ashok Leyland, the

Chennai headquartered publicly listed truck manufacturer which is majority-owned by the Hinduja family. Whilst the bulk of the Hinduja business interests lie outside India, it is in India that they usually make it to the front pages of the newspapers. Unfortunately, for Ashok Leyland's public shareholders, the Hindujas are seldom in the news for the right reasons. As a result, this is a stock that investors find hard to fall in love with in spite of the fact that this company: (a) runs several high quality plants which produce reliable trucks; (b) has the largest truck distribution network and after-sales service network in southern India; and (c) has a brand that most truckers would swear by.

However, the public's apathy for the company means that over the past decade whenever India's economy is facing headwinds, Ashok Leyland will be trailing at a hefty discount to its fair value. For the discerning investor, who is willing to look beyond the tabloids, this represents an opportunity. In each of the last two economic cycles (roughly spanning the last decade), Ashok Leyland's share price has tripled from its low point (at the bottom of the economic cycle) to its zenith (at the top of the economic boom).

Trap 3: An aversion to the unfamiliar

As Nassim (*Black Swans*) Nicholas Taleb has pointed out, our mind wants to make sense of the world around us by constantly seeking patterns and building stories of what we are seeing (even if there are no real underlying patterns or stories). Therefore, since it is easier for our mind to build patterns and stories of what is familiar, the mind prefers the familiar over the unfamiliar.

Not only is the squalid, decrepit milieu of most Indian cities unfamiliar to most FIIs (who tend to be more used to well-scrubbed money centres such as Shanghai, Manila and Hong Kong), the chaos of Indian politics and the cultural unfamiliarity of India makes it hard for investors to feel at ease about India. Thankfully, a few investors know that political chaos and squalid urban infrastructure has little to do with stock market performance. China has neither political chaos nor decrepit infrastructure and yet the Indian market has outperformed its Chinese counterpart over one, three, five, ten and twenty years!

Trap 4: Overweighing low probabilities

Our minds tend to overweigh the probability of events which have happened recently. So, for example, if you have been thinking about plane crashes (perhaps because of a recent plane crash captured graphically on TV), it will impact your beliefs about the safety of flying. Similarly, if you are exposed repeatedly to news about corruption scandals in India, it will make you think about the pervasiveness of corruption in the country. That in turn could alter your perception of the trajectory of the Indian stock market (even if there is no link between political corruption and the direction of the stock market).

What successful long-term investors have trained themselves to do is factor in the implications of these four sets of problems to protect their portfolios from these mental traps. Success in investment management is often the result of cultivating the reflective mind in such a way so that investment decisions are not compromised by the instinctive responses of the reflexive mind. To be specific, successful long-term investors exhibit the following five traits to a greater extent than the average investor:

1. Scepticism,
2. Risk aversion,
3. Openness of mind,
4. Patience and preparedness, and
5. Contrarianism.

THE SCEPTICAL MIND

'My way of avoiding falling prey to market noise—something that I follow at all times—is to think, ask questions and think again. Keep doing that.'—Prashant Jain[2]

---

[2] *Outlook Profit*, 19 March 2010 issue, pg 86.

A sceptical mind is a powerful tool that can protect investors from aggressive promoters and brokers who over-promise. I learnt this the hard way in my first year in broking in the UK. As a greenhorn, I used to call institutional investors with a 60-second pitch along the lines of, 'Buy Gee Whiz Software because they have created a CRM package which is being adopted by all the large banks. Gee Whiz's market penetration amongst banks is only 20 per cent but with Gee Whiz signing up banks at the rate of four per month, the company is set to enjoy rapid growth.'

Successful investors keep asking the question 'Why?'. So after hearing my pitch on Gee Whiz, they would ask me what was so special about the CRM package, why couldn't other vendors replicate it, had Gee Whiz generated profits and cash flow from selling these packages or was it merely signing up these banks with revenues promised some years down the road, and if the package was so promising, why had management sold 30 per cent of its stake in its IPO. At client meetings I would find that this kind of questioning would go on and on until the investor was satisfied that Gee Whiz's success was rooted in sustainable competitive advantages and the company had strong financials and a respectable promoter.

About a year into my broking career I realised that I needed to have at my finger tips around two pages of information about every stock that I pitched to investors—the first page would explain why the company in question has sustainable competitive advantages and the second page would have its key financials including its free cash flows. Based on these two pages of information, I would go to meet investors and the most seasoned amongst them would go into detail about almost every facet of the information contained in my two pages. Often I would spend three hours or more with a seasoned senior investor discussing the same stock in enormous detail. The London afternoon would often turn into night by the time I would be let out of the investor's office, exhausted but enlightened by the power of the sceptical mind. As one of my first clients taught me, *'If it sounds too good to be true, it probably is.'*

THE RISK AVERSE MIND

'My first principle is not to take on large risks. One of the things I have learned and which I believe in is that risk is best defined as "not knowing what you are doing". This is Buffett's definition of risk and is far superior to what most of us are taught in business schools.'—Sanjoy Bhattacharya[3]

Dopamine is a chemical in our brain that helps us figure out how to take actions that will result in rewards at a future date. Dopamine signals originate deep at the base of the brain, roughly where the brain connects to the spinal cord. Of the brain's roughly 100 billion neurons, well under one-thousandth of 1 per cent produce dopamine. However, as Jason Zweig points out in *Your Money and Your Brain*, these dopamine producing neurons are extremely powerful—when activated '....these neural connections shoot forth their bursts like fireworks, sending vast sprays of energy throughout the parts of the brain that turn motivations into decisions and decisions into actions. It can take as little as a twentieth of a second for these electrochemical pulses to blast their way up from the base of your brain to your decision centres.'[4]

Three researchers—Wolfram Schultz at the University of Cambridge, Read Montague at the Virginia Tech Carilon Research Institute and Peter Dayan of University College London—have made three discoveries which have helped us understand how dopamine drives risk taking behaviour:

- Getting what you expected produces no dopamine kick at all. This explains why most forms of addiction escalate because once the addict gets used to a certain level of stimulus, that stimulus does not produce a dopamine kick. Hence the addict takes a higher dose to get his next kick. In money management,

---

the addiction is risk and the 'kick' is reward. Many investors find that success leads them to take greater risks by stimulating the need for an even bigger 'high'.

- An unexpected win produces a huge dopamine kick. If you earn six times the expected value on a small cap IPO in the space of a year, then the dopamine kick gives your brain a big jolt of motivation. That in turn excites you enough to repeat the gamble.

- If an expected gain fails to materialize then dopamine dries up and this produces intense disappointment. As Jason Zweig puts it, 'It is as if someone yanked the needle away from an addict just as he was about to give himself his regular fix'.

Successful investors have trained themselves to insulate their investment decisions from the euphoria and disappointment generated by dopamine. They simply refuse to load up further on a winning investment just because the stock price is going up. Instead, they have trained themselves to do quite the opposite—sell when the stock price is surging and buy when the stock is falling—that is buy when the dopamine kick is missing (and hence when a regular investor will experience intense disappointment).

Over the years, as I have watched this pattern of behaviour among top fund managers, and seen some of them become exceedingly wealthy individuals, I have asked myself 'How do they not get addicted to this process of successfully investing and then reaping the rewards from it (in the form of huge pay packets)?' For reasons which I have not been able to pinpoint, for all their wealth, the great investors usually tend to stay relatively grounded—both in terms of their lifestyle and in terms of behaviour (in the stock market and outside it). The closest I have come to understanding the relationship between their success and their behavioural patterns is that those who got too caught in the fruits of their investment success, usually lost their way sooner rather than later.

There is another dimension to the troubles caused by dopamine for investors: the desire to make predictions. Since self-confident predictions are a fundamental pre-requisite for gambling, research has shown that the more the dopamine centres of the brain are stimulated, the greater the tendency to gamble. Hence if the first-time investor buys a stock which triples in a few months, say due to the sector in question being the flavour of the season, he usually attributes this success to his ability to make predictions. Thus emboldened, he makes even more confident predictions and invests even more money on the back of those predictions. If he's successful again, the spiral continues until, of course, the collapse of the sector, or sometimes the whole market, brings him down to earth at the cost of a big hole in his bank account. Most retail investors' behaviour in stock market booms has followed this pattern for centuries.

A noteworthy tendency of successful long-term investors is the reluctance to make bold, decisive predictions. Instead they tend to rely on the 'margin of safety'. As explained in the previous chapter, margin of safety means that you only buy the shares when the share price is at least 30 per cent below your estimate of fair value. In doing so you are cutting down the risk that: (a) your estimate of fair value is wrong; and (b) that you lose money on your investment as the stock market refuses to recognize your estimate of fair value.

The average investor, on the other hand, is not only bad at making predictions, he also has misplaced confidence in his ability to get these predictions right. Successful long-term investors avoid investments where the potential for the shares to rise largely hinges on a 'big prediction' (either about the industry or about the company) coming true. In fact, they avoid these stocks even more actively if the market is expecting these predictions to come true.

Unfortunately, scientists have not yet figured out exactly how pleasure and pain are transmitted by our brain or why 'rewards' feel so good. Hence there are no scientific answers yet as to why a small minority of successful long-term investors are able to deal with dopamine so much better than the rest of us. My personal, non-scientific, experience tells me that almost all of the successful long-term investors are calm, collected individuals who don't seem to be in rush to go anywhere or trade the market through the day. They are happy researching companies intensively and spending time travelling and thinking (rather than worrying too much about their next 'reward' fix). There are bound to be exceptions to this rule but, this has been my observation in the case for most of the successful investors that I have known.

As Hans Breiter of Harvard Medical School points out, the MRI brain scans of cocaine addicts expecting a fix and traders waiting to make a profitable financial gamble are very similar—the patterns of neurons firing are virtually identical. Successful long-term investors seem to have figured out a way to avoid this mental overheating. In the next chapter we delve deeper into whether you and I can learn to behave like the legends do. Alroy Lobo, the CIO of Kotak Mutual Fund, summarised the rational mindset of an archetypical successful long-term investor's approach in his interview with me (*Relentless Research*) when he said:

'We have changed weights in HDFC Bank also. It is a good bank but if it is too expensive then we will cut and similarly with Sun Pharmaceuticals which is a fantastic company but there are times when you get it cheap. Once there was an announcement that the company had to pay a penalty. That brought Sun's share price down and we brought more. Those are the opportunities we look for. But we will not chase a stock that is too high priced. For growth stocks we are willing to look a little more ahead. For good companies rather than only one year, we look at 2 years. But we will not discount five years...we are very disciplined... but we generally like companies that have a good returns profile... We don't mind buying companies with a low return if we believe the ROEs and ROCEs are going to be trending upwards. Similarly, we are willing to buy free cash flow negative companies if we can see the free cash flow turning positive.'

THE OPEN MIND

> *'One of the things that have helped me is that I try and speak to as many people as possible and listen to their views.'*—Prashant Jain[5]

---

[5] *Outlook Profit*, 19 March 2010 issue, pg 86.

As discussed in the previous sub-section, self-confident predictions—a pre-requisite for gambling—are driven by the dopamine centres in our brains. For fund managers this problem is even more acute since they are supposed to be experts and expected to know more than the average investor. They are much more likely than the average investor to make overconfident predictions and then trade frequently on the back of those predictions.

A key behavioural difference between successful long term-investors and average investors is that the former constituency is willing to listen to and fully consider bearish views on stocks that they own and bullish views on stocks that they have avoided. In fact, a defining trait of some of the most successful fund managers I have advised is that on all of their key holdings, they will assiduously seek out the most articulate bears and then spend hours discussing the bear case on their holdings. This ability to have open minded discussions with colleagues, advisors and brokers who don't necessarily agree with them, gives successful long-term investors the highest possible chance of avoiding costly errors.

The average investor on the other hand suffers from 'confirmation bias'—he will only listen to people or sources who agree with him that his holdings are great investments and the stocks that he does not own are perpetually condemned to be non-performers.

I remember one of India's top mutual fund managers, a manager who to this day manages a significant amount of my savings, being blindsided about the issues that we found with Crompton Greaves. All the way through 2010–2012, my colleagues and I sought to convince the fund manager and his team about the company's limitations. We used a battery of factual evidence to substantiate our bearish stance but all our presentations failed to persuade the fund manager. In fact, after most of these meetings, the fund manager would ask us 'Have you spoken to the management? What do they think of your bearish views?' The management obviously disagreed with us but that's what they are paid to do.

We—the stockbrokers and the investors—are the people who are being paid to take a dispassionate view of the company and when rationality fails us, no amount of analysis is of use.

THE PATIENT AND PREPARED MIND

'It's not that I'm so smart; it's just that I stay with problems longer.'—Albert Einstein

Diligent research followed by deep reflection takes time and more seasoned investors know this. They let investment decisions percolate in their head and then they let their subconscious mind work. As Peter Bevelin notes in *Seeking Wisdom*, 'In nearly every detective novel since the admirable stories of Conan Doyle there comes a time where the investigator has collected all the facts he needs for at least some phase of the problem. The facts often seem strange, incoherent and wholly unrelated. The great detective, however, realises that no further investigation is needed at the moment, and that focus and concentration will help discern a pattern from the facts collected. So he plays his violin, or lounges in his armchair enjoying a pipe, when suddenly, by Jove, he has it!'[6]

The other dimension of 'patience' that the investment profession rewards is the patience to let the stock price come your way. You might have identified a great business but at current prices, the stock might be overvalued (or might not have the 'margin of safety'). A successful long-term investor will wait and then wait some more until the stock price falls to a level where the shares are very significantly undervalued by the market.

Whilst successful long-term investing requires patience before pulling the trigger, it also requires disciplined research of the sort highlighted in *Chapter 2* during these periods of waiting. Doing their groundwork allows the best investors to take advantage of situations

---

[6] *Seeking Wisdom: From Darwin to Munger*, Peter Bevelin, (Post Scriptum AB, 2007), pg 217.

when the market is either too depressed or too excited about a stock. As legend has it, Warren Buffett read Anheuser-Busch's Annual Report for twenty-five years and patiently waited for the stock to become cheap enough for him to buy. Finally, in 2005 the share price dropped and Buffett purchased a major stake in the firm.

Closer home, there are certain successful and richly valued companies in India where either I or my colleagues have taken senior foreign investors for meetings repeatedly over the years. One of these investors, a British FII, has visited a Mumbai-based retailer with us for four years in a row. At each meeting, the FII asks the retailer how the last year has gone and what the retailer plans to do in the year ahead. Then when he comes out of the meeting he shares with me his notes from the meeting which are something like:

- Initiatives planned last year: 5; initiatives delivered upon 2;
- Initiatives planned for the next year 3; initiatives likely to be delivered upon 1;
- BUY if stock price falls 50 per cent to P/E of 13 times or less; otherwise AVOID.

As explained earlier in the book, successful long-term investors participate in many dozens of meetings and invest many weeks of work into making each investment decision. It is almost as if the investments NOT made are as valuable (in terms of losses avoided) as the handful of investments that are made.

THE CONTRARIAN MIND

'Another key learning over the years has been that the market or the consensus can quite often get it wrong, totally wrong. The realisation of this came to me in 2000. Virtually everyone was gung-ho on TMT stocks. Me and my colleagues had sold these in late 1999...Of course, all the sell side analysts were bullish and analysts would revise target prices every week...We did not succumb...'—Prashant Jain[7]

---

[7] *Outlook Profit*, 19 March 2010 issue, pg 86.

One of the most common ways brokers convince investors to buy stock (and store owners get customers to buy goods) is to say, *"Everybody wants this... prices are going up fast. If you want some of this, you will have to buy quickly."* The human mind is peculiarly susceptible to this simple pitch. All sorts of emotions play a part in creating this insecurity (others have but I don't), envy (others have it, I too should have it), panic (if I don't buy now, I will be left behind) and greed (if I buy it, I will get rich). Successful investors are able to avoid these emotions (and avoid falling for these sales pitches) by simply not being bothered about what others are doing.

A contrarian mind protects successful investors from the fate awaiting the rest of the herd. For example, in January 2008, after five straight years of strong returns from the Indian stock market (the January 2003—January 2008 CAGR for the Sensex was 44 per cent), the vast majority of investors were expecting strong gains. Unfortunately, in the twelve months from January 2008, the Sensex dropped by around 60 per cent. By 1 March 2009, having suffered heavy losses in the preceding twelve months, most investors did not want to be anywhere near the stock market. Instead in the 19-month period beginning March 2009, the Sensex delivered a staggering 150 per cent return (in absolute terms). Both in bull and bear markets, the average investor gets caught up in groupthink and fails to capitalise on the opportunities created by misvalued assets.

Professor Terence Odean of University of California at Berkeley says that 'The average person buys more aggressively in response to recent price rises, but not just to yesterday's big boom. What makes people buy is a combination of very recent price rises and any longer-term "trend" of rising prices that they might perceive.'[8]

A contrarian mind, because it is not tempted by the desire to join the herd, is therefore able to profit at the expense of the average investor. In the dying days of a bear market, a contrarian market is able to acquire attractive companies when they are available at bargain basement prices. At the height of a roaring bull

_____

[8] *Your Money and Your Brain*, Jason Zweig, (Simon & Schuster, 2007), pg 73.

market, even as the average investor opens bottles of champagne, the successful long-term investor books profits.

CONQUERING FEAR AND GREED

'You don't let emotion get into the process. One of my big mantras is "emotion is the enemy". Don't ever let emotion get in the way of investing. Investors fail because they let their emotions get the better of them.'—Arjun Divecha[9]

Successful long-term investors are as human as the rest of us. However, what they have mastered is how to deal with fear and greed. For example, all of us are intensely sensitive to sensory stimulus. In my case, whenever I see a can of a certain brand of aerated soft drink, I start visualizing a juicy hamburger because in my teenage years, my main form of nutrition was soft drink and burgers (they were cheap and I was broke). So now when I am travelling on work, especially in the US, I have to make it a point of avoiding aerated drinks because as soon as I have the drink, I develop an intense craving for a hamburger. You won't be surprised to know that lab tests on rats have yielded similar results—once they start associating a stimulus (say, a light being switched on) with food, even if there is no food present, the rats start getting excited.

Most investors react instinctively and emotionally to share prices especially if they are relayed on TV by loud newscasters or highlighted prominently in newspapers. Sensex plunges 300 points; banks hammered' is a typical headline which triggers fear. Similarly, 'Sensex breaches 23K, enters record territory' is a greed inducing headline. Hence professional investors ensure that they do not watch stock prices either on the stock pages of newspapers or on TV. In order to make sure that their portfolios

---

[9] *India's Money Monarchs*, Chetan Parikh, (Capitalideasonline.com, 2005), pg 130.

are managed properly whilst they are either meeting companies or conducting research, these fund managers either tell their dealers what prices to buy or sell at or they have pre-set alerts to warn them if these prices are hit. This modus operandi allows investors to stay sensitive to prices whilst avoiding the emotional messages associated with price changes.

Another way that large, successful investment firms avoid being swept away by fear and greed is by creating an investment committee. Structured properly and used effectively, such committees force a fund manager to present a dispassionate investment case to his peer group and his boss (usually the CIO). The whole process of preparing the investment case, making the presentation, getting it signed off and eventually executing the trade is intended to be long enough and thorough enough to neutralise the emotional charge associated with the investment. Even more effectively, once a fund manager starts realizing that everything he does has to be passed by the investment committee, his brain starts checking his instinctive emotional messaging. Hence the committee's effectiveness extends well beyond the time it spends deliberating investments.

'COMPANIES, EVEN THE GOOD ONES, WILL ALWAYS HAVE THEIR UPS AND DOWN'.

Sashi Reddy *is with First State Investments, the consolidated asset management business owned by the Commonwealth Bank of Australia. It currently has over US$163 billion in funds under management as at 31 December 2013. First State Stewart (part of First State Investments) which manages a range of Asia Pacific, Global Emerging Markets and worldwide and sustainability funds draws on a distinct investment philosophy which is focused on long-term investment in companies run by highly capable and highly ethical management teams. Part of First State Stewart's ethos is to focus on its investment process and its team rather than trying to cultivate star fund managers. With that ethos in mind, Sashi Reddy, a portfolio manager within the FSS team, agreed to be interviewed for this book. His views are broadly representative of what this unique investment management team stands for.*

How did you run into First State Investments ('FSI')?

SR: I was introduced to First State by a former colleague who joined the broader business within the bank. During my interview, I was asked whether *I would invest in Company X (one of India's largest private sector energy companies) given its wonderful track record?*. My interviewers gave me further evidence of the strength of the business to set me off in the wrong direction. Quite naively at the time I said 'No' as I had no strong view on the company, their track record or their returns. My response was based on my understanding of the controlling shareholders of the company. They made a virtue of 'managing the system' and it baffled me as to why we would back someone who operated this way. While it was possibly a naïve answer, especially during the bull market days of 2007, I think it was enough for the First State Stewart team to give me a chance.

The first six months in this team was an (un)learning experience! I had to dig deep into what I really believed and stood for in my personal life. I had spent time with my father working for a couple of years in his business after my graduation. He is a good investor and one of the things he did well was sticking to long-term horizons, spanning decades in many cases.

One of the trickiest parts of taking a long-term view is judging people and cultures as these are the things that really matter. Sounds simple, but is quite subjective and mind numbing at times. This is a reason why newcomers to the team can struggle at times, initially at least, as I did.

Can we delve into this a bit more—why is it a difficult thing for outsiders to do?

SR: The First State Stewart team can be a difficult place to settle into partly because of our philosophy and partly because of our process—that is the subjectivity around making some of these judgements. Agreeing to disagree, living in grey areas and not coming to conclusions are all part of our daily process! Most of us believe we will be cultural misfits in other organisations for similar reasons. Numbers are important but it is important which numbers you look at and how you interpret them. We, generally, do not believe in doing financial forecasts. We are not astrologers. We would rather go back as far as possible into a company's history to understand how managements behaved during good and bad times. This helps us understand culture, and attitude to risk and competence. Our clients are giving us their hard earned savings so that we preserve that capital and grow it over a period of time. We are looking for similar stewardship in managements of companies we invest our client's money in. Such stewards earn and maintain their license to operate every day by interacting with their stakeholders in a fair and transparent manner. This is the key to the long-term success of any business. We need to provide returns in excess of inflation to our clients in the long term. We define risk as the risk of losing money for our clients and not as deviation from any arbitrary benchmark.

Over the last 4–5 years, your credo has worked out but how did the team deal with the pressure, say 6–7 years ago, when this approach to investing was not delivering the desired results?

SR: Most of our funds tend to lag when markets are going up very strongly. These are difficult times but the danger of going down the quality curve is far higher than lagging any index! There is always 100 per cent downside when investing in a poor quality company. There are examples of this littered all over financial history. Most of our clients who have known and invested with us over cycles understand this well.

Our team's performance is measured on a rolling three- and five-year basis. This is important as we are not under pressure to deliver short term performance. We are fortunate that we have enough autonomy to operate as a boutique with control over how we remunerate the team, who we hire, decisions regarding opening or closing funds and fees, and the culture we are trying to create within our team. This autonomy is very important because it helps us take difficult decisions like closing funds. (Closing a fund means turning away new investors who might want to invest money into that fund). There is only so much quality out there and we would be harming existing clients' interests if we keep a fund open beyond its ability to invest in quality companies. It is counter intuitive but in the long term we are actually protecting our business. This business is entirely about reputation and performance.

Is your performance measured relative to a benchmark?

SR: There is a benchmark element because many clients require it. In our minds we don't worry about the benchmark. We start with a blank sheet of paper and own the 30–40 highest quality companies at reasonable valuations at any point in time. We believe if one delivers long-term performance using an absolute return mindset then the relative performance should be taken care of. Clients use benchmarks to compare us against other funds. Whilst we are not fans of this, we understand their compulsions. More importantly, we try not to allow this to affect our investment philosophy. You will never hear us talk about valuations of a company relative to an index or a sector. Our return expectations from a company are driven by the quality of managements, long term track records, strength of financials, and strength of franchise. For instance, in the shipping industry, you could have a very good management team and a good franchise but ultimately it is a cyclical industry where managers don't control their own destiny. Our expected return for such a company will always be very high. The other battle one has to fight is the artificially low rates central bankers are forcing on savers and the investment community. Think of the shipping company, why should they care about low interest rates? They could of course get cheap debt and do various things with it. But that only tells me more about their attitude to risk.

Since you joined in 2007 the size of the funds under management has doubled. That has created a need for more talent. How easy is it to find employees who agree with the team's investment philosophy?

SR: It is a challenge and should always be! Many of our team members actually do not come from the financial services industry.

Suppose five years down the road, we have in the fund management industry 20 other funds with the same approach that you have taken, will you change your approach then?

SR: We would be happy campers! We are keen to start a debate on the role of long term investing in the real world, learn and help shape behaviour where possible. The financial community's time horizons have collapsed a lot in recent decades and this has had undesirable effects on some of the practices within and outside the industry. There is a sense of privilege amongst many of its participants which needs to change. Our actions have huge implications not just for our clients but the companies we invest our client's capital in. If we provide capital to a poor quality company what message are we sending to them? The financial community is an integral part of the world's problems as suppliers of capital! Capitalism as it was practiced in the last century has many weaknesses. It is partly the reason for the unequal societies we live in today. This gap between the rich and the poor is only widening as we speak. Another weakness of capitalism is that it has taught managements to put shareholder's interests squarely ahead of all other stakeholders. This inevitably forces managements to take short cuts which can only harm the franchise longer term.

First State Stewart's investment philosophy is distinctive and it has delivered over the past decade. What are the weaknesses that you think can be addressed in the years ahead?

SR: Our approach places emphasis on identifying management teams with strong values. Companies which have to deal with regulators and governments have a certain level of opacity which we are uncomfortable with. This dilemma becomes even more acute when market leading companies in heavily regulated sectors use regulation to create barriers to entry. Such barriers obviously help the shareholders of the company but at the expense of millions of customers who end up paying higher prices than they should ideally be paying. A systemic transfer of wealth from the poor to the rich! We, as long term capital suppliers have, yet, failed to change this anomaly in many countries.

There is a risk we are sometimes cut off from the real world. Companies, even the good ones, will always have their ups and downs. The easy way out when we identify a problem with a company is to sell our shares. Managements and controlling shareholders do not have that luxury. Taking a strong view on integrity of managements and being wedded to history means there is a risk that sometimes we don't spot change quickly enough. Change does happen and such events are sometimes the strongest drivers of returns. Rooted to Scottish history, we tend to be quite valuation focused. A fall-out of this attitude is that we have sold some quality companies earlier than we should have.

FIVE

The Guru in You

'The idea that the brain is somehow fixed in early childhood, which was an idea that was very strongly believed up until fairly recently, is completely wrong. There's no evidence that the brain is somehow set and can't change after early childhood. In fact, it goes through this very large development throughout adolescence and right into the 20s and 30s, and even after that it's plastic forever; the plasticity is a baseline state, no matter how old you are.'—Sarah-Jayne Blakemore, Royal Society University Research Fellow and Professor of Cognitive Neuroscience, University College London, UK [1]

Our brain is made up of 100 billion neurons. What makes it so fascinating and powerful is that each of these neurons makes connections with 1,000 to 10,000 other neurons. Based on this information, scientists have calculated that the number of possible brain states, of permutations and combinations of brain activity, exceeds the number of elementary particles in the universe.

---

[1] The chapter on "The Adolescent Brain" in *Thinking*, edited by John Brockman, (Harper Perennial, 2013).

One of the most exciting developments in science over the past decade has been the study of how our brain works by using Magnetic Resonance Imaging (MRI). MRI scanners use strong magnetic fields and radio waves to form images of the body. The technique is widely used by doctors for medical diagnosis, staging of disease and for follow-up without exposure to radiation. Psychologists and neuroscientists have increasingly used this technique to understand how our brain performs easy tasks, such as recognizing a face, and more complex ones, such as identifying the arithmetic pattern in a series of numbers. What they have learned from these studies has changed science's understanding of how the brain works, how powerful it is and, most importantly, how 'plastic' (or malleable) it is even long after we have entered adulthood. This altered understanding of the human mind was a central reason for my deciding to write this book. But before we get into it, let's go over what it takes to be a succesful long term investor in the Indian stock market.

My decade of advising fund managers in different parts of the world suggest that the central traits, as discussed in the previous chapters, are:

1. Scepticism (but not pessimism) and curiosity;
2. Iconoclasm or contrarianism;
3. Caution and conservatism in not getting carried away by the latest fads;
4. Tenacity and persistence in trying to perform in-depth analysis; and
5. Patience (or calmness of mind) to wait for the right opportunity

For you or for me, to invest large sums of money successfully these traits are essential. To illustrate, suppose based on my ability to rigorously research stocks, I enjoy a few years of good returns and start counting my golden eggs. In that happy state, I dream of a beach house in Goa that my stocks could buy. I discuss this with my friends and they too get taken by the idea. What do you think is now most likely to happen? At the first sign of a wobble in the market, I am likely to dump my stocks after only one or two years of good returns. Some of those exits might be timely but if I really had built a high quality portfolio, my lack of patience will make that beach house in Goa the most expensive house that I will ever buy.

Hence the whole package of traits is what really helps successful investors grind out outstanding returns over two or three decades. The good news is that science has revealed over the past decade that you or I can acquire these traits provided we are willing to put in the effort, which is the 10,000 hours required, to become an expert.

The point of view that complex skills can be acquired even in advanced stages of adulthood has actually been reached independently by two different branches of science: neuroscience, which is a branch of biology and focuses on the scientific study of the nervous system, and psychology, which is, at its best, an applied discipline focusing on the study of mental functions and behaviours. Let us first explore what the neuroscientists have found.

THE NEUROSCIENTISTS' VIEW

Vilayanur Ramachandran, a California-based neuroscientist, is the Director of the Center for Brain and Cognition at the University of California-San Diego. Described by Richard Dawkins, the renowned evolutionist, as the 'Marco Polo of neuroscience", 'Ramachandran's cutting edge work, which he explains in lucid and engaging non-scientific terminology, has reshaped our perceptions of how the brain works. His work in the field has helped us understand that there is a complete map of the body surface on the surface of the brain. For every part of our body, there is a part of the brain which controls it and responds to it. It turns out that for, reasons nobody can explain, the face area of the brain is right next to the hand area of the brain.

Ramachandran found that if you remove the arm, the hand area of the brain is now devoid of sensory input. Since the hand area of the brain craves sensory input, the sensory input from the face skin (which usually goes to the adjacent face area in the brain) now invades the vacated mental territory corresponding to the missing hand. As a result, when you touch the face, the message goes not only to the face area of the brain but also to the hand area of the brain. The result: the person feels that he still has his missing limb. The significance of this result: we can see that the brain's wiring changes in response to external stimulus (in this case the loss of a limb).

Ramachandran's work, in his own words, '... *challenged the doctrine in neurology that neural connections of the brain are laid down in the fetus and in early infancy, and once they've been laid down by the genome there's nothing you can do to change these connections in the adult brain...It was believed that there was no plasticity in the brain connections. We showed in our experimenting that, in fact, there's a tremendous scope for rewiring. So much so that over a two-centimeter distance in brain tissue in the cortex the face input has now invaded the hand territory of the brain. Then we did brain imaging and showed that this invasion had actually occurred but we already knew this from the psychological experiment.'* [2]

Ramachandran's work and that of other neuroscientists like Sarah-Jayne Blakemore, are establishing that:

- Our brain adapts significantly, and sometimes dramatically, to external stimuli (a trait now defined as 'neuro-plasticity');
- Deficits, whether they be sensory (dyslexia, blindness) or physical (loss of a limb) are overcome by the brain by stimulating other human faculties; and
- Such adaptations take place not only in our formative years but continue well into our adult years.

THE PSYCHOLOGISTS' VIEW

The psychologists have approached the issue from another angle. They have sought to understand whether, by using, self-discipline we can acquire new traits, new skills and even new habits. In a

---

[2] The chapter on "Adventures in Behavioral Neurology..." by Vilayanur Ramachandran, in *Thinking*, edited by John Brockman, (Harper Perennial, 2013.)

series of celebrated studies on self-discipline conducted in the 1960s and 1970s, Walter Mischel of Stanford University showed that young children's ability to delay gratification (for example, not eating a marshmallow for long periods even though no one was stopping them from doing so) is linked to a host of other positive outcomes in later life including academic success and physical health. Furthermore, research has also shown that self-discipline is also linked to other desirable traits such as patience, impulse control and will power. Following Mischel's work, the big question which then arose is *'Is self-control a trait you are born with or is it trait that can be nurtured?'*

Psychologists do not seem to have conclusively established how self-discipline is acquired and strengthened. However, there are tantalizing hints that their research is leading them towards conclusions broadly similar to those reached by the neuroscientists:

- The early 1980s produced a major breakthrough in self-discipline theory. Professor Michael Scheier of Carnegie Mellon University and Professor Charles Carver of the University of Miami showed how self-awareness was linked to self-improvement. The two professors showed that self-awareness leads to a feedback loop according to the acronym TOTE: test, operate, test, exit. 'That is the self compares itself against the relevant standard (T), and if the current status falls short of the standard, it begins an operation (O) designed to remedy the deficit. Further tests (T) are conducted periodically. When the standard is finally met, the loop is exited (E).'[3]

- For individuals who want to achieve greater self-discipline in a specific domain, the most effective results are likely to come from greater monitoring, both by themselves and by others, of their behavior. This finding has emerged from several studies including the work done by Mark Muraven of the University at Albany. In 1999 he showed that 'people who worked on their self-regulatory capacities by daily exercises such as improving

---

[3] Chapter 22 of *Character Strengths and Virtues*, American Psychological Association, (Oxford University Press, 2004).

their posture ended up performing better than other people on laboratory test of self-control.'[4]

- Let's take a specific aspect of self-discipline: perseverance or persistence or a voluntary continuation of actions focused on a specific goal in spite of difficulties and obstacles. Psychologists are emphatic that persistence 'becomes easier and more successful with increasing age, at least up to middle adulthood.'[5] Even more interestingly, persistence is one human quality that can certainly be improved. 'A number of studies have shown that people who receive training at effort and persistence can exhibit significant improvement in their ability to persevere in the face of failure.'[6]

Broadly speaking, the findings from these two distinct branches of science point in the same direction: we can, with adequate effort, mould ourselves into the people we want to be. In fact, these findings from neuroscientists and psychologists on either side of the Atlantic Ocean help logically underpin the emphasis that popular authors like Malcolm Gladwell and Matthew Syed have put on putting in 10,000 hours of dedicated practice for those who aspire to become world champions. It is now clear that such an investment of time leads to a rewiring of the brain. It leads to the creation of new neural connections, connections that less-dedicated competitors simply do not have and hence are disadvantaged.

CHANGING NEUROLOGICAL PATHWAYS IN THE WORLD OF INVESTING

Whilst it is comforting to hear the scientists say that we have it in us to change ourselves for the better through focused practice,

---

[4] Chapter 22 of *Character Strengths and Virtues*, American Psychological Association, (Oxford University Press, 2004).

[5] Chapter 22 of *Character Strengths and Virtues*, American Psychological Association, (Oxford University Press, 2004).

[6] Chapter 10 of *Character Strengths and Virtues*, American Psychological Association, (Oxford University Press, 2004).

most of us do not have the luxury of time so that we can dedicate ourselves to the art of becoming a great investor. We live in the real world of demanding day jobs and even more demanding families. So how can people like you and I become successful long-term investors? Here is my 'cheat sheet' to investment success for those who are willing to apply themselves even for a few hours each week.

Tip 1: Have a realistic expectation of what sort of returns equities can deliver for you. On a cross-cycle basis, Indian equities will give a return broadly equal to the cost of equity in India, which is around 15 per cent. Given that this is the long-term return from Indian equities, if the Nifty has delivered far higher returns three years in a row, it is a time to start becoming circumspect and, in all likelihood, it is time to start selling. On the other hand, if for three years, the Nifty has given returns well below 15 per cent, it is probably time to start increasing your exposure to stocks. However, for you to make such rational (or contrarian) decisions, you need to have realistic expectations about returns on your investment around which you can base your buying and selling. Otherwise, you are highly likely to run after the herd and earn cross-cycle returns well below 15 per cent.

Tip 2: It helps if you don't look at the share prices of your investments frequently. Unless you have a mind which is immune to what the ticker is doing, you really should not be looking at the prices of your stocks any more than once a month (actually, once per quarter is ideal). And when you do look at prices, do so at a time when the market is shut and when you are in stable frame of mind. In fact, I would suggest that you don't watch the financial news channels or your Bloomberg/Reuters terminal during market hours. That's one way to prevent your reflex brain being tempted into poorly thought-through investment decisions. As the father of behavioural analysis and Nobel laureate, Daniel Kahneman says, 'If owning stocks is a long term project for you, following their changes constantly is a very, very bad idea. It's the worst possible thing you can do, because people are so sensitive to short-term losses. If you count your money every day, you'll be miserable.'[7]

Tip 3: Another way to protect your portfolio from your reflexive mind and its ability to make inaccurate but overconfident predictions is to diversify your portfolio—a sensible portfolio should contain at least fifteen stocks. Chosen properly (from a mix of sectors and market cap size buckets), fifteen stocks should give you protection from overexposure. Obviously, you can have many more than fifteen stocks in your portfolio if you want (most professional investors will have at least forty to fifty stocks in their portfolio) but the incremental utility (from the perspective of diversifying your portfolio) of adding stocks to your portfolio diminishes rapidly once you go north of fifteen.

Tip 4: Ask yourself 'What could go wrong?'. Rather than focusing on the current stock price and how much you think the company is worth, ask yourself 'What if the business is worth only half of what I think it is?' or 'What if the company has a reputational scandal tomorrow, can the business recover from the scandal?'. Only after you have convinced yourself that even with stock price getting trashed in the market, you can still afford to live with the downside risk, should you go ahead with the investment.

Tip 5: Take it easy. Since over-activity is not going to result in investment outperformance, there is no point in taking anything other than a measured approach to investing. A relaxed, stable mind which is unaffected by what the rest of the herd is saying is likely to be able to swim through the tides of greed and fear that sweep through the stock market. Unsurprisingly therefore, investment legends in India and elsewhere, tend to be cool, calm, collected people.

Tip 6: Lay down simple investment rules and follow them. The rules given in the previous chapters of this book (Examples: Only buy the stock if you understand the business model, only invest in companies which can generate cash flows, provide a high return on capital employed for long periods of time and so on)

---

[7] *Your Money and Your Brain*, Jason Zweig, (Simon & Schuster, 2007), pg 83.

seem to work for a number of seasoned professional investors. A similar set of rules which lay down simple parameters for what you will and will not consider for investing will be very helpful for you. Entering the stock market without such a set of rules is like setting sail without a compass (or a GPS).

THE AUTHOR AS A CASE STUDY

Like many other finance professionals, I had learnt the textbook aspects of investing—accounting analysis, competitive advantage analysis, valuation, etc—by my mid-20s. None of these facets of investing are particularly hard to learn and, at least at a superficial level, there are numerous courses and textbooks which can help a beginner understand these concepts. My challenge was, and remains, that the psychological aspects of investing were harder to understand and harder still to master.

In the three years that I spent this writing this book, I had plenty of time to think about the psychological aspects of investing. As I interviewed the Gurus and then spend weekends transcribing and polishing their interviews, I found the similarity between their psychological profiles remarkably arresting. In particular, the point that everyone I spoke with reiterated was that the best time to invest is when no one else is doing so and that struck a chord with me.

The more I have thought about this specific facet of contrarianism, the more acutely aware I have become of when the top fund managers build their biggest positions. So, for example, seeing the British fund manager build a US$100 million position in Maruti in August 2012, even as the company's share price reeled in the wake of the trade union-related tragedy in its Manesar plant, was a riveting experience (see *Simple Rules of Investing* in this book for more details). Similarly, watching a large FII build a US$100 million position in IDFC in August 2013, even as its stock price slid alongside the erosion in the value of the Indian Rupee, was a didactic experience.

In late August 2013, my new learnings were put to the test. August is usually the month when my employer pays bonuses. As a result, this ends up being the month when my wife and I review our finances. As in most middle class househsolds in Mumbai, the annual discussion usually focuses on 'Can we afford a larger apartment?' In the closing days of August 2013 we concluded, like we do every year, that we could not. The question then arose *'What should we do with our financial savings?'*

This was around the time that I had read an article in the 24 August 2013 edition of *The Economist* which echoed investors' disillusionment with India. I was greatly influenced with its hard hitting description of a paralysed country sliding down the mire. I told my wife 'Let's put half of our savings in small-mid cap equity funds.' My wife looked at me sceptically and asked me 'Are you sure about this?' I hesitated and for a moment as I thought about what would happen to our hard earned savings if the Indian economy went into freefall. Would our dreams of sending our children abroad to study be compromised by my rashness? Then I snapped out of it and said what the legends had taught me, 'The best time to invest is when no one else is doing so". Thus, in the last week of August 2013, with the Sensex at around 18,000 (down from over 20,000 in January 2013), we invested nearly half our financial assets in two small-cap mutual funds.

As I finish writing this book in August 2014, the Sensex is at 26,000, up over 40 per cent since we invested exactly a year ago. However, since we had invested in small-cap mutual funds, our August 2013 investments are up nearly 100 per cent. Now, my mutual fund broker, who was shell shocked to see me invest in small caps a year ago, calls every week to ask if I would like to buy more. I tell him what the legends told me: "I will buy when others are selling. For now, I will take profits if you don't mind."

'THERE IS FUN IN BEING A CONTRARIAN ALTHOUGH IT CAN BE RISKY'

*Having begun his career in the late 1980s with Canara Bank's nascent mutual fund, **BN Manjunath** is one of the first institutional fund managers to work in the Indian market. In 1993 he joined Lloyd George Management, one of the first FIIs to enter India, as their Chief Representative in India. From 2001 right up to his retirement in March 2014, he was an advisor for Ward Ferry Management, a firm founded by his longstanding friend, Scobie Ward. A graduate from the Birla Institute of Technology & Science (Pilani), BN Manjunath's remarkable journey mirrors India's evolution over the course of the last twenty years from the backwaters of global capitalism to one of the largest stock markets in the world.*

You are the first Indian fund manager who did not originate from UTI. How did that happen? How did you become a fund manager?

M: I am not sure if I was the first non-UTI manager in the industry; SBI probably had a couple. I first joined Canara Bank in Bangalore and I was working in the Economic Research Division. Then in 1987 the public sector banks were given permission to run mutual funds. So the bank deputed me to Mumbai to join the mutual fund and help set up the Equity Research function. Once in Mumbai, I and some other members of the team were asked to do a short term course in fundamental analysis specifically designed for the Canbank Mutual Fund staff. The course was conducted by Professor Prassanna Chandra from IIM Bangalore. It was a great initiation into investing and a wonderful learning experience on how to value stocks. This was followed by a Crisil-organised seminar for fund managers and Sanjoy Bhattacharya, who was at Crisil at that time took us through the grind. They were the earliest influencers of my thinking on the process of investing in equity markets. They gave me a direction of how exactly to go about doing this job in a systematic manner.

Then I started reading company annual reports and my learning took place on the job between 1987 and 1990. In those days there wasn't really anybody other than UTI to learn from. It was challenging but it was fun. There were hardly any fund managers in those days and there was limited direct contact with companies for fund managers. The key, I figured out, was to assess whether a company was running its business well and doing so in a consistent manner.

Did you have a mentor at Canara Bank or you were the main man when it came to equity investments?

M: On the equity research side, I was the main man in the initial two years and I was learning on the job. In hindsight, those were the days when I learnt the most. I made a lot of mistakes but even those were good learning experiences. I learnt, for example, not to get excited if a company posts good numbers for one or two years; that it is the longer term track record that matters.

In those days (1987) there were very few equity mutual funds and the equity culture hadn't really arrived in India. So how did you market your funds?

M: In Canara Bank at that time we had one growth fund and two or three income funds. In 1987, the typical Indian household was not really interested in mutual funds. To be fair, they did not know then what mutual funds were. We (the bank) marketed the funds with a team of four to five people. We would go to top metros and a few upcoming cities like Mysore, Ahmedabad, Vijaywadaa, Vishakapatnam and Hyderabad and the local bank manager would pull together a cross-section of bank customers for us to talk to. We would then explain to this audience what mutual funds were and how they worked.

What sort of corpus were you running in 1987–1988?

M: Initially I went to Mumbai to set up Canara Bank's equity research desk but I was also asked to help the debentures team and the income fund management team. That being said my core responsibility was on the equity research side. So in the initial one year I did not actually manage a fund myself. I was more involved in doing research and identifying a certain set of ideas and then the bank would decide what to do with those ideas. I was told that, to the extent possible, I should be travelling around the country looking for investment ideas rather than spending time in the office. The result was that I did a lot of travelling in my initial years.

Were you already clear in your head then that you were looking for a good management team, cash flows, ROCE, etc. or did that came much later?

M: By nature, I am conservative. So I was clear that I would not chase a flashy company. In the early years there was no pressure of competitive performance. That also helped me settle down. Also, because I was working in a bank, I knew what kind of management teams could be trusted to look after a business. So I approached the issue from a credit perspective and looked for solid, strong companies. Initially, the flows into the fund were small—I think the growth fund had at that time around ₹80 crore worth of assets. By late 1988 when I was asked to manage the growth fund, I had started settling down into the profession. Those days they were not many broking houses who did research and had strong corporate contacts. Most brokers in those days worked on tips and on operator contacts. I think there were only one or two brokers—Enam and KR Choksey come to mind immediately who tried a fundamental analysis/research based approach—in those days, and I got to know them. That said, broker research was quite basic and wouldn't by itself suffice to justify any investment. As the fund manager I would have to do the grind myself—from meeting the company, reading the annual report, punching in the figures into the calculator (there were no computers or spreadsheets then), estimating the numbers and the ratios. You built everything from scratch.

How did your philosophy change as you entered the 1990s and then India liberalised?

M: In 1990, Banque Indosuez of Paris launched a fund to invest in India called the Himalayan Fund. It had about US$75 million of assets and it was one of the earliest offshore funds to be launched for India. In those days there were two other offshore funds in the market—the UTI India Growth Fund which UTI co-managed with Merrill Lynch and the India Magnum Fund which SBI co-managed with Morgan Stanley.

The Himalayan Fund was a 10-year closed end fund aimed at investing in the Indian sub-continent. Since in those days there was no concept of FIIs, Banque Indosuez had to sign-up with a local partner, which is how Canara Bank came into the picture. The fund was based in Amsterdam and since Banque Indosuez wanted someone with a background in investment management rather than from mainstream banking to be put in charge locally, I was chosen to be the local support fund manager in July 1990. I just happened to be in the right place at the right time. Banque Indosuez's investment business was managed from Hong Kong. The head of the Hong Kong business was Mr Robert Lloyd George (who would go on to create Lloyd George Management). As far as the Himalayan Fund was concerned, apart from periodic interactions with Robert, on a more day-to-day basis I had to work with two of his colleagues: Mr Jeremy Higgs, Robert's deputy, and Mr Scobie Ward, (who would go on to found Ward Ferry Management). Scobie was my direct counterpart in Banque Indosuez and he would come down to India once a quarter and I would go to Hong Kong three to four times a year to make my presentations or for the investment management committee meetings. I learnt a lot from Scobie and from the team at Banque Indosuez. I learnt, for example, how a foreigner viewed Indian companies and how different that view was from the local view. I must also add here that Pradip Shah, who founded and was heading CRISIL at that time and was the independent director on the Himalayan Fund, was also a great help in adding to my learning in fund management and stock selection.

How does the foreign investor's perspective on India differ from that of local investors?

M: In India you get very influenced by the short term perspective; the noise, the broker reports, quarterly earnings, who are the major buyers, sellers, etc. In contrast, the foreign investors, or at least the ones I worked with, focused more on the longer term company track record, the company's fundamental strengths and weaknesses, sectoral trends and the company's longer term growth strategy. This divide between the foreign view and the domestic view has reduced now because the Indian buy side has now picked on the same learnings and Indian firms have become so much more institutionalised. But back then, local fund managers would pay a lot of attention to what UTI bought and sold. So, for example, if I really liked a company but someone told me that UTI, the big daddy, was a seller, I would then, given my inexperience, be concerned about the influence it would have on my calls. Working with Scobie and the team at Banque Indosuez taught me to ignore such peripheral knowledge!

How did your investment philosophy change through the early 1990s?

M: Those days the quality of disclosures in financial statements was not that good. So I think I made mistakes in my analysis in a few cases. The other factor which led to mistakes was meeting time deadlines for investment. What happened was that due to the first Gulf War the market had crashed as oil prices shot up and the Indian currency got a pounding. We were able to buy some good blue chips at attractive prices but during that time we had a deadline mandated by the RBI: we had to invest 70 per cent of the fund before the end of March 1991. So in that hurry maybe I did not do enough research. There was no electronic trading in those days. Apart from research, I was responsible for the Board minutes, company meeting notes, as well as settlement of trades. But I learned a lot about how a market operates. Those three years (1990–1992) gave me a real grounding in equities.

You quit Canara Bank in 1992. Why did you move given that the issues of working in the public sector, from a reputational standpoint, were well known and well accepted?

M: I decided to leave in early 1992 although I was personally happy working on the Himalayan Fund at Canara Bank. The main issue was my desire to move to a more professional, dynamic work atmosphere and move away from a hierarchical, 'public-sector' work atmosphere which prevailed at the bank and of which I had enough. Plus, Canara Bank also wanted me to manage local funds. Given that I was handling research, the offshore fund, and the settlement process for that fund, taking on domestic fund work, where I would have a relatively less decisive say, did not make sense.

There is fun in being a contrarian although it can be risky. I have had this urge since my University days and had taken contrarian decisions regarding career while in Bangalore! Although I had no place of my own in Bombay (Mumbai now) those days, and a very young—three year old daughter, I decided to quit. Perhaps that was the attitude that motivated me to make the move. I had one advantage—there was hardly anybody in India at that point of time with my sort of experience in institutional fund management and I thought opportunity would come if not soon, within a year or two. I discussed this with my father, and he too having been a sort of 'contrarian' in his personal and professional life supported my decision.

At that time SEBI was looking at expanding the domestic mutual fund industry and was working on giving permissions to private sector companies to run mutual funds. After I put in my papers at the bank on 3 January 1992, word spread to a few of the potential private sector entrants. Then I got a message from a firm called Credit Capital Finance Corporation Ltd (which had an association with Lazard, UK) on January 1992 requesting me to meet them. I met the Chairman and he said that he was applying for a mutual fund license and offered a senior position at the firm to help set up a fund. He said Lazard Asset Management and IFC Washington would be his partners and they would bring in the equity investment. I thought it was a great opportunity to get involved with a new fund and run it independently and hence took up the offer.

Once I took up that job in April 1992, the whole process of SEBI giving mutual fund licenses became very time consuming. As usual, it had to go through Parliament and the bureaucracy. In that time, I went to London to meet Lazard and met their fund managers and senior executives. I and the team at Credit Capital also met IFC executives in Bombay. Both these external investors agreed to invest equity in the asset management company but the fund could not start until the Parliamentary sign-off. The fund managers I met at Lazard became good friends and some of my best learnings over the years came from them.

Six months passed and the Parliament did not sign-off and that meant I had nothing to do. Meanwhile Robert Lloyd George and Scobie Ward left Banque Indosuez and set up their own firm, Lloyd George Management. They contacted me to ask whether I would become the Indian advisor for their funds. So in 1993 I moved to become the Chief Representative in India of Lloyd George Management, a position I held until March 2000.

Once you began your new innings in Lloyd George did you see the world differently and invest differently compared to your years at Canara Bank?

M: Yes. The first two years were very interesting. At that time we were very bullish as everything looked good in 1993. We bought a lot of great companies but we also bought a number of companies that I would not go anywhere near now. We had five or six sugar stocks, three or four packaging companies. The good news was that was the year of 'sugar & packaging' and because of that we ended in the top funds list in Asia. The bad news was that next year we were in the bottom quartile as we could not exit the sugar stocks before the whole sector went down. After that we learnt a lesson: not to be too exposed to sectors where the government has a big role. Also that was a time when many other FIIs were entering in and we felt the need to deploy our cash quickly. So, I learnt that when you are in a hurry to invest, you go down from 'A grade' to 'B grade' stocks and then from 'B grade' to 'C grade'

In those early days of FII investing, the investor did not forgive you if you sat on cash. So we were under pressure to deploy the funds quickly. We paid the price for this rapid deployment in 1995–1996. Even then we were learning a few useful lessons. We had invested in Infosys, Hindustan Lever and Punjab Tractors to begin with. A few other holdings of ours like Sundaram Fasteners, Bajaj Auto were also doing well. So gradually the lesson dawned on us that success is a matter of picking up good companies and not really worrying too much about the macro call. Since then the only two macro variables I have been concerned about are interest rates and the exchange rate.

Most investors obsess about economic growth. Why do you believe that interest rates are more important than economic growth?

M: I will give you an example. In December 2011 I decided to look back and study how the Indian markets have done over a long period. Since I had been in fund management since the mid/ late eighties and more directly from 1990, I took March 1992 as a reference point. In March 1992, the Sensex closed around 4285. That was the first full year of the so-called 'liberalisation'.

Now the 20-year compounded annual rate of return on the Sensex between March 1992 and March 2012 (when the Sensex closed around 17,000) just about kept pace with Real GDP CAGR in the same period of about 7.5 per cent. Adjusted for currency depreciation, the returns have been even more disappointing. In other words, despite India substantially liberalising and in spite of the growth of mutual funds, participation of a number of FIIs, private sector insurance companies, better access to research, electronic trading, etc. the stock market on the whole has not really been much of a wealth creator or matched returns from fixed income-bank deposits for example. Having looked at these returns I have come to understand and respect why the average Indian household does not invest in the stock market.

The correlation between GDP growth and stock market is not that strong and I came to the conclusion long ago that the only macro drivers that I should pay more attention to are the two (interest rates and exchange rates) that actually directly influence the P&L. More importantly, my focus is on healthy, sustainable ROCEs and ROEs. Sustainable ROCEs in excess of the weighted average cost of capital is essential and businesses which can generate these returns without having to visit the market to raise fresh equity frequently will compound very well. At any point in time, you can point to two dozen companies in the BSE500 which will meet these criteria.

I will give you an example. Last year I went down to Chennai and I met this company called Sundaram Finance, an NBFC that listed in 1972-73. This is the only company to the best of my knowledge that has grown its loan book 14-15 per cent, compounded over four decades without ever raising capital. Over the four decades, the share price, adjusted for bonus and dividends, has done phenomenally well for those shareholders who stuck with it. If I am not wrong, it is the only listed financial services company, including banks, in all of Asia which has not raised capital again. And nobody covers the stock!

Tell me more about other influencers of your investing style.

M: As mentioned earlier I had a great learning experience when I went to London in 1992 as an employee of Credit Capital to meet Lazard Asset Management. There amongst the Lazard fund managers I met was Patrica Maxwell-Arnot. She was one of the best pan European fund managers at that time. She said that while picking stocks she too favoured companies with respectable ROEs and ROCEs, good business practices and management quality. So I said that 'this management quality' thing is very subjective. Do you have any way to make an objective assessment of the quality of management?

She responded that 'it is an interesting question' and she took some time to respond. She said that this issue of subjectivity can be addressed by three very simple questions: (1)What does the management say it will do, (2) Does it do what it says it would do, and (3) How does it do what it says it will do. I thought it was brilliantly put. I haven't seen it as well articulated in any other book. When I read an annual report, especially the 'Management Discussion and Analysis' part of the report, I keep Patricia's three questions in mind.

So these three questions gave you a rational framework within which to assess management quality?

M: When I came back to India from that trip to London, I actually collected sixty annual reports and went through them. I had plenty of time as the fund was yet to start. It was a very instructive exercise for me. I only found four companies which actually stated clearly what they would do and how they would do it. I found over the years that there is a strong correlation between management teams which clearly say what they will do and how they will do it and the generation of free cash flow and ROCE.

The irony was that I came back to India in 1992 with this learning and in 1993 I started working on the Lloyd George funds. Since we had a time-bound imperative to invest and I got swayed by the exciting 'big picture' theme of investment in India by FIIs, I myself did not follow the discipline this process entailed. I was not diligent enough. I should have spent some more time following this process.

Over the last 15–20 years, if you had to choose two or three companies which said that they will do straight forward sensible things, have done straight forward sensible things and have shown the ROCE and the cash flows from these initiatives, which companies would you choose?

M: Infosys had done a lot of proactive work until recently but they were also part of a sector which had a lot of tailwind. So it was relatively easy for the Indian IT services industry to flourish in the late 1990s. TCS is as good an example as any of sustained long term performance and ability to do well even in downturns. If you take a very long period of 10-15 years, some of the MNCs fall in this bucket. Bosch, for instance—has been a fabulous stock despite the cyclicality of the sector. Exide Industries has done well, at least until 2009-2010. Godrej Consumer has done well over the last ten years. So has Titan. Hero Moto Corp, Bajaj Auto, Sun Pharma, CRISIL are other examples. In Financial Services, HDFC Bank, HDFC and Shriram Transport (until a couple of years ago), have done a great job. There are a number of other examples too, I am sure one can find which match these requirements.

How do you strike a balance between building conviction about a stock and yet keeping your mind open that you might be wrong?

M: What I came around to building is a framework where I have to assess four risks about a stock: business risk, management risk, liquidity risk and valuation risk. I am OK with business risk because a good management team will figure out how to deal with it. I can think of stocks where I could see that there was a temporary downturn in the sector but also that the management was dealing with the downturn. I am fine with that. Liquidity risk is also OK because if over a period of time a company performs, liquidity stops being an issue. Valuation risk is also fine with me—I am willing to buy a good company at what the market perceives to be a premium valuation as long as the management is delivering the requisite ROEs and ROCEs.

The critical risk which is hard to deal with is management risk. Once I lose faith in management, say due to high management churn at the senior level, corporate governance concerns, reckless diversifications, etc. it is hard for me to revisit a stock and I take a long time to even consider them for study. Infosys, Crompton Greaves, UB Group are relevant examples in this regard—for different reasons though! May be I am not as open-minded on this issue as some others are or I should be. Being more open-minded on this particular point is a continuing but difficult lesson for me!

How do you know when to sell a stock that you are holding?

M: That is the most interesting question of any discussion on investment management. Where I get more things wrong even today, it is on the selling side rather than the buying side. It is relatively easy to identify stocks to buy if you are willing to do the legwork of travelling, meeting competitors, customers, etc. Selling, however, is hard. I and most of the team I have worked with have developed a culture over the years that if a stock has done well, and the company as well as the sector continues to have growth drivers in place with the added management comfort in place, then there is a great reluctance to sell. I think it is easier to live with 'perceived' high valuations in such cases. We don't want to make the mistake of selling a good company just because it is temporarily perceived as overvalued. Even if the stock is actually richly valued, I think it need not be a straightforward 'sell' because the quality of the company's management might be better than anything the peer group has to offer. I am open to taking such valuation risk if it results in lower management risk. So when you ask this question about selling discipline, to me even after twenty five years of being in investment management, this is the biggest challenge.

Many Indian promoters need significant amounts of political connectivity to get things done. How do you judge a promoter who is working with the help of a politician?

M: I was bought up in a certain way and with a certain innate 'conservatism'. My father gave me an interesting early insight or view that if any company is doing extraordinarily well in India— much more so than anybody else is doing—one of two things have to happen: either the sector itself is booming and hence the leader is flourishing or the company is cutting corners and not doing it straight. In either case the sustainability of the firm's success is questionable. That was my father's view—it may be rigid but it keeps coming back to my mind. In my career I have tried to avoid politically connected stocks, more so post 2001. I do not recommend that the fund buy such stocks even when these stocks have boomed or the business cycle may be turning positive for them. As you can imagine, this means that there is a big list of corporate groups that I have left alone in my career.

Then how do you deal with sectors such as power, infrastructure and real estate?

M: Simply by staying out of them. Very rarely, if at all, I may decide to study them. In fact, wherever it makes sense, I have generally been advising them as 'potential shorts'.

What is your criterion for identifying a big short?

M: I learnt a few very useful lessons in 2008–2009 when I thought the banking sector was heading for problems and that restructuring would be far more severe than the market was assuming. There were a few short calls on some of the wellknown banks, the so-called good banks on grounds that their valuations were too rich. All of these shorts went wrong. After that I learnt that you cannot short stocks in India based only on valuation. There has to be a structural catalyst or a management quality issue. There has to be something else which hits the company's numbers.

'THIS BUSINESS REWARDS SOMEONE WHO IS PATIENT RATHER THAN SOMEONE WHO NEEDS A QUICK FIX'

Anonymous *was until recently the Chief Investment Officer of one of India's most prestigious mutual fund houses. Sanjoy Bhattacharya, whose interview is featured in Chapter 1, once told me that "if there is one fund manager who I will give my money to manage, it is this man". I have personally invested heavily in anonymous' funds and have found the returns to be more than satisfactory. Unfortunately, the Public Relations department of Anonymous' erstwhile employer does not want his name to be associated with this interview. However, given the sheer depth of the insights that Anonymous has provided, I decided to go ahead and publish the interview without revealing his name. In the few years that I have spent in the Indian market, I have benefited enormously from this investment legend's willingness to share his wisdom and his experiences. It is only fair, that others, especially the future generations, too get a chance to hear the great man's thoughts.*

Twenty years ago, when you began your career in fund management, how did your investment philosophy begin to develop?

A: When I entered the investment management profession, I had the academic background to at least distinguish the companies which delivered value in the long run. As a result, within a few years of being in the profession, my focus was totally on free cash flow generation and return on capital employed as opposed to other metrics. Having said that I have to tell you that the other day we were interviewing an analyst and this guy had the same kind of a background as I had when I entered the market. He had also probably had read the same kind of financial literature that I had. And inspite of all that education, he said the only way to make money in the stock market is to have inside information. It was shocking to hear that because it implies that almost your entire education amounts to nothing the moment you enter the investment management profession and you start getting impacted by by day-to-day information.

In the 1990s, you avoided the worst of the tech boom's high flying stocks which later fell to earth. How were you able to do that?

A: We had a fairly high exposure to tech companies. What we avoided was a certain type of company...the tech boom meant that a lot of companies with very questionable business models and questionable promoters had entered the market just to get a valuation even though they had no underlying business as such. The mistakes we made in the initial phase of the 1990s helped us avoid promoters who didn't have a proper business case. So when the crash came we were disproportionately invested in the better quality companies. These companies also corrected as they too were probably overvalued at that point of time but at least these companies had solid business models and a long term business case. Hence these companies did not disappear. We focused on avoiding companies that disappeared, companies which took people for a ride. This helped us avoid mistakes not just in IT but in other sectors as well.

What helped us in the late 1990s was the lessons we had learnt from the IPO boom of the early 1990s. Because of the mistakes we made in that IPO phase, we learnt the need to avoid companies which did not have a history. We learnt the importance of avoiding new issues or promoters who did not have a long enough track record. We may have missed on some of the better quality companies which were new to their sectors but our aim was to avoid big mistakes rather than to identify emerging winner companies. We were willing to sit out the initial phase of a company's growth and make sure that the promoters were genuine rather than go with the untested and untried promoters and thereby make mistakes.

Is this philosophy still maintained when you assess IPOs?

A: Fortunately for us many of the IPOs' valuations over the last many years have been so high that it did not make any sense to look at them. So even if we liked the company, the valuation at which they were hitting the market was way beyond what we were willing to pay.

Let's go back to the interesting point you raised about this analyst you were interviewing. What do you think predisposes so many market participants towards the inside information rather than the fundamentals of the company?

A: It is a difficult question to answer. My personal view is that in a country like India, people who gravitate towards the stock market are relatively well qualified people...people who probably should be focussing their attention on something else rather than the stock market. These type of people need to see rapid results. However, this business rewards someone who is patient rather than someone who needs a quick fix. Because these guys are restless and the fact that many of these guys are intelligent, they think that they can do that much better relative to the broader market. Hence they tend to take a lot of shortcuts which they feel will probably convert their ideas into money quickly. I think the game is as far as investment management is concerned is to stick to a few basic tenets and follow those with patience.

Things will evolve in India. The investment management profession in India has a fairly short history. Until ten years ago only a very tiny group of people invested in the Indian stock market. The middle class was totally unexposed to the stock market. It is only in the last ten years that people who have been formally trained in investment analysis have started entering the investment management profession in India. Gradually, as a broader, deeper class of well-trained market professionals emerges, this obsession with short-term trading and inside information should moderate.

In the boom years running up to 2008, were you able to stick to your approach of long-term investing focused on fundamental quality or was there any change?

A: We stuck to our investment philosophy and it hurt us in the boom years of 2006–2007. Because of the way we do our research and value our analysts' opinions, they push us to look at long term investment ideas. As a result, even if a stock is doing very well in the market, unless we are convinced of the underlying fundamental merits, we always come to the conclusion that it doesn't make sense from a long-term point of view.

Let's look at a 'fundamental' argument, which had a lot of supporters during the 2006–2010 phase. India needs infrastructure. However, companies which build this infrastructure, can't be expected to generate cash flow quickly. So it's unrealistic for you as an analyst to be looking for infrastructure stocks which generate cash and healthy ROCEs. In fact by focusing on such metrics, you will miss out on a growth opportunity. How did you deal with this line of argument in the boom years?

A: What we did was looked at companies which were a play on infrastructure but which were not directly classified as infrastructure, for example, the banking sector. Of course in banking we made the distinction between public sector banks and the private banks and we wanted to avoid public sector banks at all cost. Generally, during a boom, a lot of mistakes are made in terms of lending and hence we stuck to the private banks. Also when we saw the infrastructure boom we focused on companies which despite being classified as capital goods had a compelling case to be deemed 'infra'. Take Cummins India for example. It is a good way to play shortage of power in the country and I can't remember the last time it raised fresh capital. So we focused on companies like that. We zeroed in on companies which had some credibility in the management. We avoided many of the contractors and the infra asset owners who had leveraged balance sheets.

How do you assess what is a good management team in an industry like infrastructure where promoters necessarily have to deal with politicians and the government?

A: Many of us had experiences earlier either as lenders or as employees of some of these companies. Having seen these infra companies at close quarters, we clearly did not see value in many of the infrastructure business models which were coming up. We thought the best way to play this sector would be through IDFC where the promoter pedigree was good. We thought that in terms of analysing the infrastructure space IDFC had all the right business models. IDFC was a monoline business with exposure only to infrastructure.

You said you have invested heavily in the banking sector. How do you evaluate banks given that the standard metrics of cash flow and ROCE can't really be applied to banks?

A: We have always adapted to that. Within our team, there are two schools of thought on this subject. Firstly, you pay for quality and at least in the growth phase of the Indian economy, quality has delivered. Quality banks have continued to grow despite their higher valuations. At the same time we have tried to see whether we should invest in banks which had a cheaper valuation because of lower ROEs. Whilst we have made a few such investments, in the long run these investments have by and large not delivered. So the better quality banks with higher ROEs have continued to deliver better value in the last ten years than private banks.

So 'value investing' in financial services stocks does not work?

A: Value investing in financial services stocks hasn't worked in India. In fact, value investing in financial services comes with its attendant set of risks. Most of these entities are naturally leveraged. As a result, if you have invested in a cheaper bank, the adverse impact of sub-standard credit appraisal skills can be very high. Therefore, when you see a bank trading at a low valuation multiple that is the market's way of saying that the credit appraisal skills of that lender might not be quite what it should be.

So how does one decide at what valuation a bank is overvalued? Is the correct price:book multiple for a well-managed bank 2x or 3x or 4x?

A: As long as a bank's growth rate is holding up and provided you are comfortable with the business model and its risk profile, I think you are better off buying a bank which is still growing quite aggressively but trades at a high price:book. For such a bank, the day its growth rate falls, there is going to be sharp derating.

SM: A core tenet of your investment philosophy is that certain promoters will deliver in the long run and you prefer to back such promoters. Given how the Indian market suffers from speculative bubbles, such a philosophy would have given you long periods of underperformance. What was the longest such period of underperformance and how did you deal with that?

A: In the previous boom which climaxed in early 2008, we had a long period of underperformance from late 2005 to 2008. The underperformance was huge and it was mainly because some of the sectors which were doing well were unfortunately not sectors about which we had a great deal of conviction.

We found that we were not good with certain kinds of investments, for example, betting on cyclical stocks which require timing the entry and the exit. Even if we had a liking for a certain sector, if the fundamentals did not merit investing in that sector, we stayed away.

We stayed away from the Real Estate sector which did very well in those years. It was very tough for us because we are managing the public's money. We were being compared by benchmarks and peers on a regular basis and there are pressures internally. We also have to market our funds to the public. But I think what we have realized, and some of our peers have also realized, is that as long as you stick to the basics, it all evens out in the long run and the better quality portfolio generally tends to do well.

To a certain extent being able to deal with underperformance depends on the kind of firm you are working for. Our philosophy is that we need to make investments based on sound logic and in-depth research. That research leads us back to good management teams and good businesses and, over the long term we believe this approach delivers investment performance. I think for a fund manager there needs to be backing from his firm for that sort of approach to investing. The kind of firm you work for is also important.

What happened to your fund flows in those two to three years (2005 though to early 2008)?

A: Until the middle of 2007 all mutual funds, including us, saw good flows. Then towards the end of 2007 our fund flows reduced sharply because of our underperformance. In absolute terms we did not lose money. In terms of the relative performance the flow of money obviously gravitated towards certain other types of funds. A lot of infra funds became very large.

Can we now look at the other type of difficulty that investors face—buying a stock which you regret and which had a bearing on your broad approach to investing?

A: Most of the good quality companies that we have bought, we still hold them in many of our portfolios. However, in some cases we exited some of the good companies on the premise that on a relative valuation basis, there was more value elsewhere. We really regret those mistakes because we now understand that a good quality business may become expensive for a period of time and you probably have to sit out that period; maybe allow that investment to underperform. The natural approach to take for a fund manager is to say 'I will sell now and keep the stock on my radar so that I can buy it back when it is cheaper.' That is easy to say but the problem is that when the stock gets cheaper, fund managers generally do not act on their self-stated premise. So if you own a good business which is doing well but the stock price is probably running ahead of fundamentals, in long run it is best to continue holding such stocks. HDFC Bank is an example of such a stock.

Beyond that, as far as mistakes are concerned we make too many mistakes, so it will be difficult to make a list. For example, the Media sector is something where we thought there was great potential. Unfortunately, if you look at the kind of companies from that sector you don't have too much of choice. So we ended up backing a TV channel which from the business perspective seems to have done very well but from a shareholder perspective hasn't really delivered to our expectations.

A number of investors seem to take the view that well-educated professionals who go on to set up businesses make better promoters. Do you agree with that?

A: Our experience of investing highlights the fallacious nature of this line of thinking. I have seen, and this is my personal view and not my firm's that in India professional teams somehow seem to take more short cuts than some of the older business families. People seem to assume that education means better ethics but that doesn't seem to be the case in India at least. Many of us tend to assume that the guy who is well educated will do the right thing but that's not necessarily the case.

How about private equity? What do you make of businesses which have private equity firms sitting on the Board?

A: Private equity in India is actually bad for investors. If you look at the listed space and the private equity space, I think the quality of the listed space is far superior to the private equity space. I understand that to generate higher returns, the private equity firms have to take more risk but the quality of business evaluation is much higher in the public space and as a result, the quality of companies is higher in the public space.

I think private equity funds' need to generate their higher returns sometimes results in them putting the cart before the horse—they end up investing in capital consumptive businesses hoping that the business will prosper one day.

My view is that you cannot set a target return and work towards that. That is not possible. The returns will happen. If you do a good job of investing in well-managed companies, you will get the sort of good returns that the economy can give you. You cannot put the return in your spreadsheet and work backwards.

How do you focus on what you think is essential for your investment analysis and cut out the rest of the noise?

A: We have a core list of companies which we track systematically and irrespective of the kind of inputs we get, we stick to that core. The core list obviously does not have companies where the promoter's integrity is in question or the business model is in question. Having said that we also don't want to be static given that the Indian economy is evolving and we are bound to encounter new business models. Moreover, in the last twenty years we have seen a lot of businesses evolving, so we don't want to shut ourselves to new businesses. So what we have tried to do is to build some dynamism in this core portfolio.

We have now got an analyst who looks at new ideas especially in the midcap space. This analyst's job is to bring these ideas to our fund managers' attention but we are extremely careful about any of these new ideas. We ensure that we do enough diligence on these ideas. Again, this caution is informed by the past. We have learned that in looking at new ideas, we made big mistakes. So we want to be careful when we look at some of the new ideas. Having said that, Telecom was a new idea ten years back and now it is one of key sectors of the market. We want to have a portfolio which focuses on the core ideas but also has some dynamism built-in so that we don't miss out on new ideas.

One part of your job is to develop conviction in an idea. Another part of your job is to keep yourself open to the possibility that either you might have got your call on a stock wrong. How do you strike a balance between these two conflicting pressures?

A: It's not that we have not made mistakes and there have been times when we have gone horribly wrong but the aim is to minimise mistakes. The aim is to reduce the impact of these mistakes on the portfolio. So now what we do is when we have a new idea we add a little bit of that to the portfolio, watch how the investment performs and then build on it.

A very different type of challenge arises with our large investments. For example, we have a large exposure to the Telecom sector and we have been holding it for I don't know how many years. As you know, the sector has been going through a series of regulatory challenges which have impacted the fundamentals of the business and the valuations of the stocks in that sector. Throughout this process of regulatory churn, we kept going back to our Telecom analyst. After all, the sector has been a huge underperformer in the portfolio and we are massively overweight relative to the benchmark. Again and again we have gone back to the drawing board, tried to see where we have gone wrong and tried to assess whether we need to take any corrective actions. So far we have stuck to our exposure despite the fact that it's been a huge underperformer but we keep revisiting the investment and re-examining what we should do.

Within the firm there are people who are more conservative than the others in terms of exposure. So even if one of our colleagues likes the stock a lot, there are some of us who limit our exposure to a certain level.

I understand how your firm can make stable long term investments rather than ride these cycles of fear and greed but is there some other driver you think that allows fund managers to stay focused on the long run rather than be driven by fear and greed?

A: If you have a core set of beliefs in terms of what value is, you tend to do less and less with the portfolio. That in turn will then allow you to take a more detached view of what is happening in the market on a day-to-day basis. Finally, regardless of how intelligent you are, if the ticker is going to trouble you then I don't think you have the right aptitude to be a portfolio manager. I think people who have done very well with investments do very little with their investments! The problem with many of us is that we think that we know everything about every sector. We should stick to the sectors where our knowledge is relatively better. There is information overload I think we need to ensure that we do not get overloaded by this information. You don't need to know everything about a company. Many analysts are mistaken that the moment they know everything about a company, they know how the company's valuation will move. I think what you need to understand is what drives that business' value rather than the day-to-day headlines that impact the business.

I think people who run investment boutiques are in a better position in that they can sit back and take a long term call and I think they are less impacted by the day-to-day pressure. They have a smaller set of clients whom they know very well they can probably deliver better value to those clients. An individual investor can probably deliver better value than a portfolio manager. In fact, an individual who knows his risk appetite and his holding period I think has an edge over the professional investor.

Acknowledgements

Most of us growing up in middle class Indian families are accustomed to seeing our parents grind out a living. Even in the context of this embattled milieu, I reckon my parents took more hard knocks than most, both in India and in the UK, to give my sister and myself the best upbringing they could. To them I owe my education and my conviction that life has to be lived for a whole lot more than a large bank account.

In my professional life, there are three large intellectual debts that I feel duty bound to acknowledge. John Kay, whose firm—London Economics—was my first employer when I graduated from the London School of Economics, taught me the utility of thinking for oneself rather than believing in conventional wisdom. Steve Norton, one of my managers during my days as a management consultant at Accenture, taught me to how to think and write in a structured manner. Nick Paulson-Ellis gave me a chance to enter the world of stockbroking when he founded Clear Capital in a flat in south London and allowed me to be a co-founder.

In the few years that I have worked in the Indian stock market, I have learnt extensively from the fund managers interviewed in this book. Beyond the gurus featured in the book, the three other fund managers to whom I am grateful for helping me appreciate specific facets of fund management are Kenneth Andrade, Zaheer Sitabkhan and Soumendra Nath Lahiri. Just as importantly, practical lessons in the art of survival in the bowels of the Indian stock market have come from my friends, Alok Vajpeyi and Anirudha Dutta.

Whilst there are several good books on Western fund managers, this genre is not yet popular outside the West. Hence well-written material on Emerging Market fund managers is hard to come by. In this context, I have found two publications to be very useful. The first is a set of interviews conducted with Indian fund managers in 2005 and compiled into a book called *India's Money Monarchs* by Chetan Parikh, a distinguished money manager himself. The second is a special issue of a now defunct magazine called *Outlook Profit*. This issue was published on 19 March 2010 and contained unusually insightful interviews with several Indian fund managers.

My employer, Ambit Capital, allowed me to write this book in spite of knowing that it could detract from the amount of time and attention I could devote to my day job. My thanks to Rahul Gupta and Ashok Wadhwa for their understanding in this regard.

Several colleagues helped me research portions of this book. I am particularly grateful to Karan Khanna, Gaurav Mehta, Pratik Singhania, Parita Ashar, Rakshit Ranjan, Ritika Mankar-Mukherjee, Pankaj Agarwal, Nitin Bhasin, Bhargav Buddhadev, Dayanand Mittal and Ashvin Shetty for their help. I also thank Ankur Rudra for his help in the decade that we worked together.

I come now to the "home team", the three people who bore the opportunity cost of the many weekends that I spent hunched over my laptop trying to coax this book into shape. My children—Jeet and Malini—and my wife—Sarbani—bore my tantrums and my frowns as I fretted my way through the chapters. Without their love and support I would neither have been able to finish this book nor survive the rigours of the stockmarket for as long as I have done. I dedicate this book to them and I promise them that I will not begin writing a book for another year.

This book would not have been written had Arundhuti Dasgupta Singhal of *Business Standard Books* not reached out to me and then prodded me over a three-year period to get the job done. I thank her for keeping me focused on the book even as I grappled with the existential pressures of managing a brokerage in a bear market.

Finally, my thanks to the support staff at Ambit—from those who serve us beverages to those who keep our working environment pleasant to those who proudly hoist the tri-colour on the terrace of Ambit House every morning. All of them contribute to making our working lives that much more enjoyable. Hence it is only appropriate that all the royalties from this book should go to the Oditi Foundation, the not-for-profit set up by Ambit for its support staff.

About the Author

Saurabh Mukherjea is CEO of the Institutional Equities business at Ambit. One of the top three analysts in India according to Asiamoney 2013, Saurabh has spent most of the past decade making sense of the chaos that surrounds the Indian stockmarket. A London School of Economics alumnus and a CFA charterholder, Saurabh lives in Mumbai with his wife and two children.